Mustards, Pickles and Chutneys

MARGARET O'SULLIVAN

AURUM PRESS

ACKNOWLEDGEMENTS

With thanks to all the good friends who delved into their recipe collections, particularly Marie Toshack and her family of country cooks, also Ros Bowden, Joan Edison, Jean Higgins, Keith McLean, John Sears, and Renate Yates.

First published in Great Britain 1992 by Aurum Press Ltd,
10 Museum Street, London WC1A 1JS
Copyright © Collins Angus & Robertson Publishers Pty Limited 1991

A catalogue record for this book is available from the British Library.

ISBN 1 85410 215 X

10 9 8 7 6 5 4 3 2 1
1996 1995 1994 1993 1992

First published in Australia by Collins Angus & Robertson Publishers Pty Limited

Cover photography by Scott Cameron

Printed in Australia by Griffin Press Ltd

CONTENTS

$\mathscr{I}$NTRODUCTION

Making mustards, pickles and chutneys is an art that we shouldn't allow to die out. Thanks to a new generation of chefs who are reviving old skills, it seems unlikely that it will. These young innovators are adapting our grandmothers' ideas and inventing new ones; creating fresh chutneys to go with exquisite designer food, and pickling exotic delights to stimulate conversation as much as the tastebuds.

Preserving is essentially a country tradition: country home-makers have always tried to be as self-sufficient as possible, and that means storing the bounty of summer produce for the leaner times in winter. It's a way of thinking that is increasingly popular in today's conservation-conscious environment. While freezers have lessened the need for other forms of home preserving, making pickles and chutneys is still a satisfying and rewarding leisure pursuit. It takes the original fruit or vegetable into another dimension that is complementary to fresh or frozen food.

Why make your own? Well, there is a world of difference between bought and home-made, and not only in the taste. When you make your own, you know exactly what you are getting. And the range can be so much greater than the selection at your local supermarket. Specialty shops sometimes stock a good variety, but prices are high. You can make your own for a fraction of the price—and double the satisfaction. Home-made preserves make delightful gifts, too.

We associate home preserving with big country kitchens, but you can do just as well in a tiny city kitchen. The equipment is basic—you probably have almost everything you need already. It's one area of cooking where it doesn't hurt to improvise. No need to go out and buy special jars—save jars and ask friends to save theirs as well. And don't be afraid to experiment: if you want to change a spice, or if you hate a particular flavour and want to leave it out, that's fine. Changing the type of vinegar is also unlikely to have drastic consequences. Certain principles, outlined at the beginning of each section, should be observed, but in general, pickling and chutney making isn't as exact a form of cooking as, say, cake making.

You will be amazed at how easy it is to make your own mustards and pickles, and how little time it takes. Making chutney is a slower process, but also simple. It's a soothing pursuit in a high pressure age. And the rewards are great: gleaming jars of produce that turn simple fare into a banquet.

A NOTE ON SPICES

Chillies: Chillies in various forms are used throughout this book as an important flavouring. It may be useful to keep in mind the following tips when cooking with chillies so that flavouring can be adjusted to suit personal tastes.

Fresh chillies: Fresh chillies come in a variety of sizes and flavours but as a general rule, the smaller the chilli the hotter the flavour—seek the advice of your greengrocer.

When cutting chillies it is best to wear rubber gloves or cut them under cold running water as irritation can occur. The seeds of chillies can be extremely hot and are usually discarded.

Chilli powder: Chilli powders can vary in strength from pure ground chilli to chillies blended with other spices resulting in a milder flavour (Mexican-style chilli powders fall into this category).

Curry powder: Curry powder can also be bought in varying strengths from mild to hot. Use according to taste.

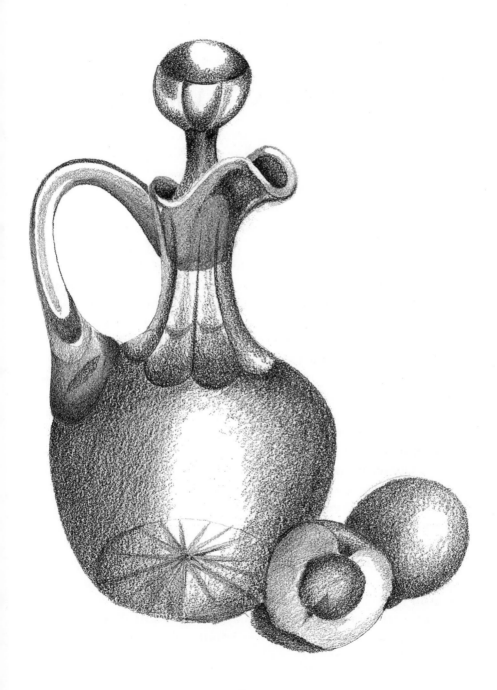

$\mathcal{M}$USTARDS

In recent years we've discovered a whole range of new uses for mustard. Char-grilling, for instance, has created a demand for all sorts of condiments, particularly mustard. But there's nothing new about its popularity. We're a long way behind stout trenchermen of the Middle Ages who ate it by the gallon. In those days a nobleman's household could easily consume 200 gallons a year (914 litres in today's terms)—not surprising when you consider that at one banquet 50 guests might easily get through half-a-gallon (2285 ml). One of the reasons for its popularity was that it helped to disguise the taste of rancid meat! Nowadays we value it as the perfect partner for ham and roast beef, and for its ability to add bite to sauces, pickles and dishes such as Welsh Rarebit. Added to mayonnaise and salad dressings, it helps to stabilise the emulsion as well as giving a flavour boost.

Mustard plants have been cultivated for more than 2000 years. Before later generations discovered it could be ground to a paste, the ancient Egyptians chewed the seeds with meat. Mustard plants also crop up frequently in Biblical, Greek and Roman writings, where the seeds were used medicinally—certainly by Hippocrates and probably earlier.

Mustard is the name of a family of plants (Cruciferae) whose flowers have petals in the shape of a cross. There are three main types: white mustard (*Brassica alba*), which is actually a yellowish colour and has the mildest flavour; black mustard (*Brassica nigra*), actually dark brown, with a spicier flavour; and Indian or brown mustard (*Brassica juncea*), the strongest.

Mustard powder, as we know it today, was first made by an Englishwoman called Mrs Clements in 1720. Until then all mustards were of the grainy type. She ground the seeds in a mill, rather than with a mortar and pestle, then sieved the powder to remove the hulls. Her discovery found favour with King George I, and was soon made commercially throughout the country. It was known as Durham mustard—a tribute to Mrs Clement's home town. In 1814 a miller, Jeremiah Colman, bought a flower and mustard mill in Norwich where he produced this type of mustard powder. Later he bought a factory in Carrow exclusively for the production of his popular mustard; Colman's famous mustard is still made in that factory.

Today, English mustard powder consists of ground black and white mustard seeds, wheat flour and spices. It is mixed with cold water to make traditional English mustard. The water must be cold as heat destroys the enzyme that gives mustard its pungent flavour. Vinegar and salt also inhibit the enzyme's development, although you can add them after allowing the mustard and water mixture to stand for 10–15 minutes, without any loss of flavour. Mix English mustard 10–15 minutes before serving to allow the full flavour to develop. Do not keep for more than a few hours, or it will lose heat.

When cooking with mustard, add it towards the end and heat gently. If you want to make a milder, but slightly bitter mustard, you can substitute vinegar, beer, cider, wine, or even fruit juice for water, when mixing the paste. Whatever liquid you use, start with a small quantity of powder, about 2–2½ tablespoons in a small dish, and gradually add the liquid, a teaspoon at a time, mixing to a smooth paste. Don't make too much at a time: mustard manufacturers make their profits on what gets thrown away!

While the English like to make their own mustard, the French and most other Europeans prefer mixed mustards. Dijon is probably the best and most versatile. It's a smooth, pale yellow paste made by crushing hulled black seeds into a yellow powder and mixing with spices, salt and either white wine, verjuice (juice of unripened grapes), or vinegar. By law, no other ingredient, such as flour, oil, sugar or colouring, can be added if it is to be labelled Dijon mustard. It's good with steak, and is ideal for adding to sauces and salad dressings. A dash of Dijon mustard, added with cream to pan juices, makes an excellent quick sauce for pan-fried chicken breasts.

Grainy mustards, like those made prior to the 18th century, are still popular. Bordeaux mustard is the other great mustard of France. It's darker than Dijon, with a grainy texture and has a sweet-sour flavour due to the addition of sugar and vinegar as well as herbs and spices. Most German mustards are in this style. In general, the flavour of grainy mustards is milder than most smooth mustards—sometimes honey or sugar is added to produce a sweet mustard. These mustards go well with frankfurters and other sausages.

It's easy to make your own mustard by grinding mustard seeds (I use a coffee grinder that I keep strictly for spices) and mixing with water, spices, herbs and other flavourings.

NOTE: *Sugar in a recipe refers to white granulated sugar unless another type is specified.*

Basic Mustard

50 g (2 oz) black mustard seeds
50 g (2 oz) white mustard seeds

Water
1 teaspoon salt
White wine vinegar

Grind the mustard seeds in a coffee grinder if you have one, otherwise use a mortar and pestle. Put into a bowl with enough water to moisten, leave for 10 minutes, then add the salt, stir, and put into a jar with enough white wine vinegar to cover. Cover the jar and leave for 1 week, then drain off the excess liquid.

Cover again and store in a cool, dark place. It will keep well for several months. You can vary the flavour by adding other spices or herbs with the vinegar. And you can make a milder mustard (and stretch the quantity) by adding some flour with the salt.

Apricot Mustard

The fruity flavours of this apricot mustard go well with barbecued chicken and pork spareribs.

100 g (4 oz) mustard powder
1 tablespoon finely chopped (minced) dried apricots

3 teaspoons sherry
1 teaspoon salt
½ cup (4 fl oz) apricot nectar

Mix all ingredients in a blender or food processor. It can be used immediately.

Curry Mustard

Try a dollop of this stirred into a mixture of mayonnaise, apricot jam, chutney, and either sour cream or yoghurt (yogurt). Use as a coating for cold, poached chicken—a good buffet dish.

100 g (4 oz) mustard powder
6 teaspoons curry powder (see p. 2)
1 teaspoon turmeric
1 teaspoon salt

1 teaspoon ground ginger
¼ cup (2 fl oz) olive oil
¹/₃ cup (2½ fl oz) vinegar (any kind is suitable)

Mix all ingredients thoroughly—adding a little more vinegar if necessary. Leave for 1 week before using.

◆

The term curry comes from the Tamil word kari which means sauce.

Chilli Mustard

Packs a punch with hot dogs!

100 g (4 oz) mustard powder
3 teaspoons chilli powder (see p. 2)
1 teaspoon salt
6 teaspoons sugar

25 g (1 oz) flour
¼ cup (2 fl oz) vinegar (any kind is suitable)
¼ cup (2 fl oz) vegetable oil

Mix all ingredients, except the oil, in a blender or food processor, then add the oil gradually. Keep for 1 week before using.

Lavender Mustard

There is more to lavender than a sweet smell—dried lavender can be delicious as a cooking ingredient. But it must be English lavender (*Lavandula angustifolia 'Vera'*) with grey foliage and fragrant blue/ mauve flowers. It can replace the traditional rosemary with roast lamb, stimulating conversation as well as the tastebuds. It's also good in cakes and biscuits (but don't overdo it—the flavour is potent) and this unusual mustard.

50 g (2 oz) white mustard seeds
100 g (4 oz) black mustard seeds
Water
3 teaspoons dried English lavender flowers

3 teaspoons dried tarragon
1 teaspoon salt
3 teaspoons honey
1 cup (8 fl oz) cider vinegar

Grind the mustard seeds in a coffee grinder and put into a bowl with enough water to moisten. Leave for 10 minutes. Put into a food processor with the rest of the ingredients and blend, adding more vinegar if necessary. Scrape into a jar and keep for 1 week before using.

Dill Mustard Dressing

This dressing, which has the consistency of mayonnaise, is the perfect accompaniment to char-grilled tuna—and it's a visual delight, as well as a taste sensation, with smoked salmon or gravlax (see page 5).

45 ml (1½ fl oz) white
 wine vinegar
36 g (1¼ oz) sugar
1 cup (8 fl oz) olive oil

½ cup (4 oz) Dijon
 mustard
1/3 cup (2½ oz) fresh
 dill

Mix the vinegar and sugar in a food processor until the sugar has dissolved. Gradually add the olive oil until well incorporated, then add the mustard and dill (the quantity of dill does not have to be exact, so you can simply chop off the coarse stems and put whole sprays into the processor). Pour into a jar, cover, and store in the refrigerator.

Green Pepper Mustard

One of the classic flavoured mustards.

50 g (2 oz) black
 mustard seeds
50 g (2 oz) white
 mustard seeds
25 g (1 oz) green
 peppercorns

Water
1 teaspoon ground
 turmeric
1 teaspoon salt
White wine vinegar

Grind the mustard seeds and green peppercorns in a coffee grinder or mortar and pestle. Put into a bowl with enough water to moisten, and leave for 10 minutes. Add the turmeric and salt, then mix in enough white wine vinegar to make a paste and put into a jar. Leave for at least 1 week before using.

Herb Mustard

You can vary the herbs in this mustard, depending on what you have in the garden—or can find at the greengrocer's.

*100 g (4 oz) mustard
   powder
3 teaspoons sugar
6 teaspoons fresh
   parsley
6 teaspoons fresh
   sage*

*6 teaspoons fresh
   lemon thyme
1 teaspoon salt
1/3 cup (2½ oz) cider
   vinegar
1/3 cup (2½ oz) olive oil*

Mix all ingredients, except the olive oil, in a food processor until the sugar has dissolved, then add the olive oil gradually until incorporated. Keep for 1 week before using.

Tarragon Mustard

Tarragon is one of the most compatible herbs with mustard.

*100 g (4 oz) black
   mustard seeds
Water
1 tablespoon dried
   tarragon*

*6 teaspoons flour
1 teaspoon salt
3 teaspoons honey
½ cup (4 fl oz)
   tarragon vinegar*

Grind the mustard seeds in a coffee grinder. Put into a bowl with enough water to moisten and leave for 10 minutes. Put the mustard into a blender or food processor with the rest of the ingredients and blend thoroughly. Keep for 1 week before using.

Mustard Oregano

Use as a tangy coating for racks of lamb (4 cutlets (chops) per rack): remove all but a thin layer of fat, coat with mustard, and cook in a moderately hot oven for 40 minutes.

¼ cup (2 fl oz) Dijon
mustard

3 teaspoons dried oregano
30 ml (1 fl oz) soy sauce

Mix all ingredients together. Put into a jar and store in the refrigerator.

Mustard Tomato Spread

Good with hamburgers.

*¹/₃ cup (2½ fl oz)
Dijon mustard
3 teaspoons finely
chopped (minced)
fresh parsley
3 teaspoons finely
chopped (minced)
fresh oregano
(wild marjoram)*

*3 teaspoons tomato
paste (puree)
30 ml (1 fl oz) white
vinegar*

Mix all the ingredients together. It is ready to use immediately or can be kept in the fridge until required.

Malayan Mustard

Next time you roast a big piece of beef for a party, try coating it with this spicy paste before putting it into the oven.

*225 g (½ lb) mustard
seeds
3 teaspoons finely
chopped (minced)
fresh ginger
(ginger root)*

*2 teaspoons crushed
dried chillies (see p. 2)
4 cloves finely chopped
(minced) fresh garlic
Vinegar (any kind is
suitable)*

Mix all the ingredients with enough vinegar to make a paste and simmer in a pan for 10 minutes.

Oriental Mustard

100 g (4 oz) black
*   mustard seeds*
2 teaspoons
*   coriander seeds*

2 teaspoons ground
*   cumin*
Water
3 teaspoons soy sauce
Cider vinegar

Grind the mustard and coriander seeds in a coffee grinder (if using a mortar and pestle, substitute ground coriander). Put into a bowl, add the cumin, moisten with a little water and leave for 10 minutes. Mix in the soy sauce and add enough cider vinegar to make a paste. Put into a jar and leave for at least 1 week before using.

Crunchy Mustard

100 g (4 oz) white
*   mustard seeds*
100 g (4 oz) black
*   mustard seeds*
1 teaspoon black
*   peppercorns*
3 blades mace (if
*   unavailable 3 tea-*
*   spoons ground mace)*

1 teaspoon fennel
*   seeds*
1 dried chilli
1 teaspoon coriander
*   seeds*
Cider vinegar

Grind the spices in a coffee grinder, then add enough cider vinegar to make a paste. Keep for 1 week before using.

ICKLES

Pickling is one of the easiest ways of preserving vegetables and fruit. You can also pickle other foods, such as eggs, nuts and fish. In some cases, only a few minutes work is involved and the result is rewarding: exotic treats that will help transform ordinary, even bland, food into a taste sensation as well as a visual delight.

One of the nicest things about pickles is that they look so good. Put some pickles on your plate—a pickled julienne of vegetables as a garnish, a pile of pickled asparagus on a platter of smoked salmon, and immediately you have a dish that looks as delectable as it tastes. Generally fruit and vegetables are kept whole or cut into pieces that are recognisable in the finished preserve—and this is what makes them so attractive. Most require little cooking, the exception is some fruit pickles.

Traditional vegetable pickles are made in two simple stages. First the vegetables are soaked in brine (a salt and water solution) or layered with dry salt, and left for 24 hours. Brine is more commonly used, but dry salt gives a very crisp pickle and is better for anything with a high water content, such as cucumbers. Salt acts as a preservative by a complicated process of osmosis. Moisture is drawn quickly out of the tissues of the vegetables (or fruit), while the salt flows gradually into the tissues to replace it.

Use plain, pure cooking salt. Table salt contains additives to make it run freely in damp weather, which can result in cloudy pickles, while the iodine in iodised salt darkens pickles.

To make brine: dissolve 100 g (4 oz) salt to every 5 cups (40 fl oz) boiling water and allow to cool before using. Vegetables must be completely covered with brine, so use a plate topped by a weight, to hold them under. If using dry salt, sprinkle each layer of vegetables generously; about 1 tablespoon salt to each 500 g (1 lb) vegetables.

After salting, the vegetables should be rinsed in cold water and drained well, then packed into jars and covered with spiced vinegar. Any variety of vinegar can be used—malt, white distilled, white wine, red wine, apple cider—but it must be of good quality with an acetic acid content of at least 5 per cent. Home-made vinegars are not suitable because they may have a low acetic acid content, which will allow bacteria to form. Spices are usually added whole, as ground spices form a sediment at the bottom of the jar.

These basic spiced vinegars can be made in advance and kept until needed. Use cold except when a soft pickle is desired, in which case pour hot over the vegetables or fruit.

Make sure that the vegetables or fruit are completely covered with the pickling solution; fruit absorbs liquid, so keep any leftover solution to top up jars. Make sure the cover is airtight as vinegar evaporates quickly. Don't use metal lids unless they are lined with plastic so there is no contact between the vinegar and the metal.

To prepare the jars: wash thoroughly, then place (not touching each other), while still wet, in the oven before turning on to the lowest temperature. Leave for about 20 minutes until dry. Pack the vegetables and fruit into dry, warm jars. Label with the type of pickle and the date made, and store in a cool dark place. All pickles must be stored in the fridge after opening.

Points to Remember:
• Use good quality ingredients—the fresher the better.
• Use pure, plain cooking salt without additives—not table salt.
• Use vinegar with an acetic acid content of at least 5 per cent. Most commercial brands are fine, but don't use home-made vinegar.
• Do not use copper, brass or iron cooking utensils.
• Use a wooden spoon.

• Wash the jars thoroughly, then dry and warm in a slow oven.

• Do not use metal lids unless they have a vinegar proof lining. Plastic lids or glass-topped preserving jars are ideal.

• Make sure that the pickles are completely covered with the pickling solution. Top up jars during storing if necessary.

• Most pickles are at their peak after about 6 weeks, and most are best eaten within 3 months. Some pickles are definitely for short-term use, and this is stipulated in recipes.

• After opening, pickles must be stored in the fridge.

• Vegetable pickles that have not been salted first or pickles preserved in a diluted vinegar solution will not last as long as pickles preserved in the traditional way. However, traditional techniques can overwhelm delicate flavours so other methods are used when appropriate, with the resulting shorter shelf-life.

NOTE: *Sugar in a recipe refers to white granulated sugar unless another type is specified.*

It is preferable to use blades of mace rather than ground mace for pickles, as ground mace will cloud the liquid and spoil the appearance of the pickle.

Tip: A few grape leaves packed into a jar of pickles (cucumber pickles, for instance) will help keep them crisp.

Hot Spiced Vinegar

5 cups (40 fl oz)
vinegar
25 g (1 oz) mustard
seeds
25 g (1 oz) black
peppercorns

6 teaspoons allspice
berries (Jamaican
pepper)
6 teaspoons whole
dried chillies
(see p. 2)

Method: see Mild Spiced Vinegar (p. 17).

Mild Spiced Vinegar

5 cups (40 fl oz)
    vinegar
Stick of cinnamon
3 teaspoons allspice
    berries (Jamaican
    pepper)
5 cm (2 inch) piece of
    peeled and bruised
    fresh ginger
    (ginger root)

1 teaspoon black
    peppercorns
4 blades mace (if
    unavailable omit)
3 bay leaves

Bring the vinegar and spices to the boil, then remove immediately from the heat. Cover with a lid and leave for 3 hours, then strain and use or bottle to use as required.

NOTE: *For two other methods of making spiced vinegar see page 45.*

Apple Pickle

This pickle makes a spicy change from the traditional apple sauce normally served with roast pork.

1 kg (2 lb) apples	*500 g (1 lb) sugar*
5 cups (40 fl oz) cider	*1 teaspoon cloves*
vinegar	*1 cinnamon stick*

Peel, core and quarter the apples. Bring the vinegar, sugar and spices to the boil, stirring to dissolve the sugar. Simmer for 20 minutes, strain off the spices, then return the liquid to the saucepan. Add the apples and simmer for another 5 minutes. Pack the apples into jars, cover completely with hot syrup, seal and store.

Spiced Crab Apples

Delicious with baked ham or boiled bacon.

2 kg (4 lb) crab	*2.5 cm (1 inch) piece*
apples	*fresh ginger*
4 cups (2 lb) sugar	*(ginger root), bruised*
1 cup (8 fl oz) cider	*1 cinnamon stick*
vinegar	*6 cloves*

Wash the crab apples, trim at blossom end, and put into a preserving pan with barely enough water to cover. Bring to the boil and simmer for 10 minutes. Drain, reserving 1 cup (8 fl oz) liquid.

Put the liquid back into the preserving pan with the remaining ingredients, bring to the boil, and simmer for 5 minutes. Add the crab apples and simmer until tender. Use a slotted spoon to lift the crab apples into jars, then boil the syrup for another few minutes, cool slightly and pour it over the crab apples. Seal.

Makes about 2 kg (4 lb)

Pickled Cherries

Perfect with pork.

1 kg (2 lb) Morello *(sour) cherries*	*2.5 cm (1 inch)* *cinnamon stick*
3 cloves	*1½ cups (12 fl oz)*
1 teaspoon roughly	*white wine vinegar*
chopped fresh ginger	*2 cups (1 lb) sugar*
(ginger root)	

Wash the cherries and remove the stems. Tie the spices in a muslin (cheesecloth) bag and put in a saucepan with the vinegar and sugar. Bring to the boil, stirring to dissolve the sugar. Add the cherries, cover and cook until tender. Strain the cherries and pack into jars. Return the vinegar to the saucepan and bring to the boil again, simmer uncovered until the liquid reduces to a syrup. Pour over the cherries and seal when cool.

Makes about 1½ kg (3 lb)

Pickled Bananas

An excellent accompaniment to curry.

1 cup (8 fl oz) cider
    vinegar
2 cups (1 lb) sugar
Grated rind of 1
    lemon
2 blades mace (if
    unavailable 2
    teaspoons ground
    mace—see p 16)

6 cloves
1 teaspoon white
    peppercorns
8 bananas

Bring the vinegar, sugar, lemon rind, and spices to the boil, stirring to dissolve the sugar. Simmer for 10 minutes. Meanwhile, peel and slice the bananas and put into jars. Cover with the hot liquid, and seal when cool.

Makes about 1½ kg (3 lb)

Italian Fruit Mustard Pickles

This is a simplified version of a traditional pickle. The original version requires each fruit to be cooked separately.

1 kg (2 lb) mixed
    fruit (apricots,
    plums, peaches,
    cherries, nectarines
    are all suitable)
1 cup (8 fl oz) water

3 cups (1½ lb) sugar
¾ cup (6 fl oz) white
    wine vinegar
36 g (1½ oz) mustard
    powder

Prepare the fruit: wash, remove stones or pits, and chop—in the case of plums, peaches and nectarines, plunge into boiling water, then remove the skins. Bring the water and 2 cups (1 lb) of the sugar to the boil, stirring to dissolve the sugar, then add the fruit. Simmer for about 10 minutes or until the fruit is soft, but not mushy. Set aside to cool.

Bring the vinegar and remaining sugar to the boil and simmer for 5 minutes. Set aside to cool. Stir in the mustard powder, then mix this syrup into the fruit. Ladle into jars, making sure that the fruit is covered with syrup before sealing. Ready to use in 1 week, but will keep for several months.

Makes about 2 kg (4 lb)

Spiced Figs

Succulent, spicy figs are fantastic with cheese and terrines.

2 cups (16 fl oz) white wine vinegar	4 blades mace (if unavailable 4 teaspoons ground mace—see p. 16)
2.5 cm (1 inch) piece of fresh ginger (ginger root), bruised	2 cups (1 lb) sugar
3 teaspoons allspice berries (Jamaican pepper)	Cloves 1 kg (2 lb) fresh figs Juice of 1 lemon

Bring the vinegar, spices (except for cloves) and sugar to the boil, and simmer for 5 minutes. Push one clove into each fig, add figs to the syrup, return to the boil, then remove from the heat. Allow to stand overnight, then using a slotted spoon, transfer the figs to jars. Return the syrup to the boil, add the lemon juice, then strain it over the figs to completely cover. Seal while hot.

Makes about 1½ kg (3 lb)

———— ◆ ————

Try fresh figs with cream cheese or with yoghurt and honey.

Pickled Chillies

One way of always having chillies on hand when you need them. Blanch as many chillies as you wish (toss them into a saucepan of boiling water and when it returns to the boil, remove from the heat and drain) and pack into a jar. Prepare the following spiced vinegar:

2½ cups (20 fl oz)
    vinegar (any kind
    is suitable) ˙
½ cup (4 oz) sugar
3 teaspoons black
    peppercorns

3 teaspoons mustard
    seeds, either black
    or white
2.5 cm (1 inch) piece
    fresh ginger (ginger
    root), bruised

Bring all ingredients to the boil, simmer for 5 minutes. Cool, then strain and pour over blanched chillies.

Pickled Grapes

Delectable with fish, poultry, and game, as well as an interesting and unusual accompaniment to curry.

1 kg (2 lb) seedless
    grapes
3 cups (1½ lb) sugar
3 cups (24 fl oz) white
    wine vinegar

6 allspice berries
    (Jamaican peppers)
Cinnamon sticks—
    1 for each jar

Remove stems from the grapes and pack into jars. Put the sugar, vinegar and allspice berries into a saucepan, bring to the boil, stirring to dissolve the sugar. Simmer for 5 minutes, then strain and pour the syrup over the grapes. Add a cinnamon stick to each jar. Seal when cold. Leave for 1 month before using.

Makes about 2 kg (4 lb)

NOTE: *For more visual appeal you can bottle the grapes in small bunches, but in this case you may need more syrup.*

Pickled Honeydew Melon

There is no infallible way to judge the ripeness of a melon and this is an excellent recipe to have on hand when you buy one that isn't quite ripe enough. But don't wait until then—go out and find one that's green and hard. The delicate flavour is perfect with cold smoked chicken.

1 under-ripe
honeydew melon
2 cups (1 lb) sugar
Juice of 3 limes
½ cup (4 fl oz) water
1 teaspoon black
peppercorns

1 teaspoon allspice
berries (Jamaican
peppers)
2 cinnamon sticks
1 sliced lime

Halve the melon, remove the seeds, and make melon balls. Bring the other ingredients, except the sliced lime, to the boil, stirring to dissolve the sugar. Simmer for a few minutes. Add the melon balls and return to the boil, then immediately remove the balls with a slotted spoon and put them into jars. Put 2-3 slices of lime into each jar. Fill the jars with syrup, dividing the spices as evenly as possible. Cover and seal.

Makes about 1 kg (2 lb)

Pickled Lemons

Good with couscous and other Middle Eastern dishes.

Lemons
Salt
Paprika

Ground coriander
Vegetable oil

Wash the lemons and slice. Layer the lemons, sprinkled with salt, in a colander and leave for at least 24 hours—the skins should be starting to soften. Remove as much of the salt as possible without washing, then arrange the lemon slices in jars, sprinkling with paprika and ground coriander. Cover completely with vegetable oil—if the lemons are not completely covered with oil, mould will form. Seal the jar. They will be ready to eat after about 3 weeks.

Indian Lime Pickle

A hot version of this popular pickle.

10 limes
50 g (2 oz) salt
10 fresh chillies,
  seeded (see p. 2)
6 teaspoons finely
  chopped (minced)
  fresh ginger
  (ginger root)

½ cup (4 fl oz) fresh
  lime juice

Cut the limes into quarters and remove the seeds. Arrange a layer of limes on the bottom of a large jar. Sprinkle with salt and add a couple of chillies and some of the ginger. Keeping half of the salt in reserve, repeat the layering process until all the limes are used. Add the lime juice and shake the jar to settle the contents. Cover with a clean cloth tied in place with string.

Place the jar on a sunny windowsill (or any place where all sides of the jar will get some sun) for 1 week, adding a little of the remaining salt each day. Shake the jar a few times a day. After a week the pickle can be covered with a lid and kept in a cupboard. Continue to shake the jar every day. After 10 days, it will be ready to eat with curry.

Makes about 1 kg (2 lb)

Pickled Limes

One of the traditional accompaniments to curry. Try them with couscous too.

1 kg (2 lb) limes   *White vinegar*
50 g (2 oz) salt

Wash and dry the fruit and cut into quarters on a plate to catch the juice. Remove the seeds. Pack the limes into a jar with the juice, sprinkling between each layer with salt. Cover with the vinegar, seal and shake the jar. Keep in a sunny place, and shake daily for 1 week, then store in a cupboard for 3 months before using.

Makes about 1½ kg (3 lb)

Spiced Mangoes

A mild sweet pickling liquid is used so that the luscious flavour of the mangoes isn't overwhelmed—good with any cold meat, particularly poultry.

6 teaspoons cloves	*1 teaspoon black*
6 teaspoons allspice	*peppercorns*
berries (Jamaican	*2 cups (16 fl oz)*
peppers)	*white wine vinegar*
3 blades of mace (if	*6 cups (3 lb) sugar*
unavailable 3	*1 cup (8 fl oz) water*
teaspoons ground	*6 mangoes, not too*
mace—see p. 16)	*ripe, sliced*

Tie the spices in a muslin (cheesecloth) bag. Place in a saucepan with the vinegar, sugar and water, bring slowly to the boil, stirring to dissolve the sugar. Simmer for 5 minutes. Add the sliced mangoes, return to the boil and simmer for another 5 minutes. Lift out the mangoes and put into jars. Remove the spices from the liquid and pour over the fruit. Cool and seal.

Makes about 1½ kg (3 lb)

Spiced Orange

The fragrant spiciness of these orange slices goes particularly well with duck, but try them also as a dessert with cream or ice-cream.

3 large oranges, cut	*1 cup (8 oz) sugar*
into thick slices	*1 cup (8 fl oz) honey*
Water	*1 cinnamon stick*

Halve the orange slices and simmer in enough water to cover for about 20 minutes or until tender. Drain and let stand for several hours. Combine the sugar, honey and cinnamon in a saucepan and bring to the boil, add the orange slices and simmer for 30 minutes.

Arrange the orange slices in jars. Break the cinnamon stick and divide between the jars and cover with hot syrup. Ready for immediate use.

Makes about 1 kg (2 lb)

Pickled Plums

1 kg (2 lb) plums	*4 allspice berries*
2½ cups (20 fl oz)	*(Jamaican peppers)*
malt vinegar	*2.5 cm (1 inch)*
½ cup (4 oz) soft dark	*cinnamon stick*
brown sugar	*Rind of half lemon*
4 cloves	

Wash the plums and remove the stalks. Put the vinegar and sugar into a saucepan. Tie the spices and lemon rind in a muslin (cheesecloth) bag and add it to the saucepan. Bring to the boil and simmer for 20 minutes. Place the plums in a bowl and cover with the syrup. Cover the bowl with a clean tea towel and set aside for 24 hours.

Next day, drain the plums and return the syrup to the saucepan. Reheat until boiling, then pour the syrup over the plums again. Cover and set aside for another 24 hours.

Next day, drain the plums and pack them into jars. Return the syrup to the saucepan, reheat until boiling, remove the bag of spices, and pour the syrup over the plums. Seal.

Makes about 2 kg (4 lb)

NOTE: *You can also make pickled peaches and nectarines using this method. In the case of peaches, first plunge into boiling water for about 30 seconds, then remove the skins, halve and remove the stones (pits). Substitute white wine vinegar and white sugar for these lighter coloured fruits.*

Pickled Pawpaw (Papaya)

Perfect with pan-fried fish—the seeds are decorative and can be eaten too.

*1 large green
    pawpaw (papaya)
½ cup (4 fl oz) white
    wine vinegar
½ cup (4 fl oz) white
    wine
1 cup (8 oz) sugar
1 teaspoon salt*

*2 fresh chillies (see
    p. 2)
3 teaspoons finely
    chopped (minced)
    fresh ginger
    (ginger root)
1 cinnamon stick
1 bay leaf*

Peel the pawpaw, then cut into cubes, saving the seeds. Bring the vinegar, wine, sugar and spices to the boil, then add the pawpaw—including the seeds. Simmer for about 15 minutes. Pack the pawpaw into jars, then cover completely with the hot liquid, distributing the spices and seeds as evenly as possible. Ready to eat after 1 week.

Makes about 1½ kg (3 lb)

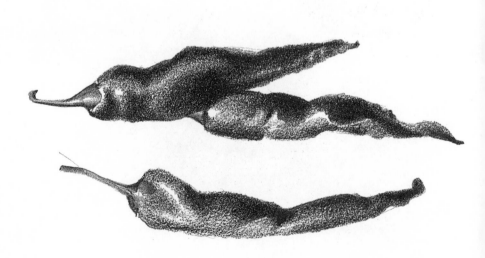

Pickled Pears

2½ cups (20 fl oz) white vinegar	Peeled rind of 1 lemon
6 cloves	1 kg (2 lb) small
1 cinnamon stick	pears, peeled,
12 allspice berries	quartered and cored
(Jamaican peppers)	2 cups (1 lb) sugar

Put the vinegar, spices and lemon rind into a saucepan, bring to the boil and simmer for 5 minutes. Add the pears, bring back to the boil, and cook until just tender, about 10 to 15 minutes.

Lift out the pears with a slotted spoon and pack into jars. Add the sugar to the vinegar and dissolve over a low heat. Bring the syrup to the boil, then pour it into the jars over the pears, covering the fruit completely. Seal and store for 2 months before using.

Makes about 2 kg (4 lb)

Pickled Prunes

One of the simplest pickles to make. Superb with ham—they're also delicious wrapped in bacon, skewered and barbecued with kidneys.

1 kg (2 lb) large prunes	1 cup (8 oz) sugar
Cold tea	½ teaspoon nutmeg
2½ cups (20 fl oz) malt vinegar	1 teaspoon black pepper
	30 ml (1½ fl oz) brandy

Soak the prunes in cold tea overnight. Next day, drain well and pack into jars. Bring the vinegar, sugar and spices to the boil, stirring to dissolve the sugar, and simmer for about 5 minutes. Add the brandy and pour the hot liquid over the prunes. Cover and seal when cool. Can be used after 1 month, but will keep much longer.

Makes about 2 kg (4 lb)

Pickled Quinces

Great with roast lamb or pork.

1 kg (2 lbs) ripe
quinces, peeled,
cored and sliced
2½ cups (20 fl oz)
cider vinegar
1½ cups (12 oz) sugar
Grated rind of 1
lemon
6 cloves

2 teaspoons allspice
berries (Jamaican
peppers)
2.5 cm (1 inch) piece
of fresh ginger
(ginger root),
crushed
1 teaspoon black
peppercorns

Put the quinces into a bowl of salted water. Bring the vinegar and sugar to the boil, stirring to dissolve the sugar. Stir in the lemon rind, then tie the spices in a muslin (cheesecloth) bag and add to the vinegar. Simmer for 5 minutes, then add the drained quinces and cook slowly until they have softened (about 15 minutes). Remove the spice bag and pack the quinces tightly into jars. Cover with the hot vinegar mixture and seal. Keep for at least 2 weeks before using.

Makes about 2 kg (4 lb)

Pickled Walnuts

A traditional Christmas treat, and sensational with cheese.

500 g (1 lb) young
green (unripe)
walnuts
Brine—50 g (2 oz)
salt to 2½ cups
(20 fl oz) water

2½ cups (20 fl oz)
mild spiced
vinegar—use either
of the recipes on
p. 17 or p. 45.

Walnuts for pickling must be used before the hard, outer skin has begun to form on them. Use a pin to prick the walnuts all over, then put them into a bowl. Cover with brine and leave for a week. Drain, then leave in fresh brine for another week.

Drain well, dry and spread on a tray covered with a clean tea towel. Keep in a dry airy place for 2 days, turning them occasionally, until the nuts are dry and black. Pack into jars and cover with hot spiced vinegar. Seal and store for at least 1 month before using.

Makes about 1 kg (2 lb)

Tutti-frutti

You can add to a crock of brandied fruit as different fruit comes into season. Spoon over puddings or ice-cream, or serve with meat—excellent with duck or baked ham. Because the fruit isn't cooked it needs to be stored in a cool place, so unless you have a cool cellar, keep it in the fridge.

Suitable fruits are:

Peaches, sliced   *Raspberries*
Apricots, sliced   *Gooseberries*
Nectarines, sliced   *Red- or black-*
Strawberries   *currants*
Cherries, seeded

Pour about 5 cups (40 fl oz) of brandy into a stoneware crock with a heavy lid or a glass jar with a close-fitting lid. Add a selection of the above fruit and the same weight in sugar. Seal. Stir daily. As you add more fruit, add the same amount of sugar, as well as more brandy if necessary (the fruit should be covered with liquid).

Pickled Watermelon (Tiger Melon) Rind

No need for any waste next time you buy a watermelon (tiger melon)—the rind makes a lovely crisp pickle that is excellent with cold meat or cheese.

2 kg (4 lb)
watermelon (tiger
melon) rind
Brine—100 g (4 oz)
salt dissolved in 5
cups (40 fl oz) water
2 cups (16 fl oz)
water

4 cups (2 lb) sugar
3 cups (24 fl oz)
white vinegar
3 cinnamon sticks
3 teaspoons cloves

Peel the skin off the rind and cut off the pink fruit. Cut the rind into 2 cm (slightly less than an inch) cubes and soak in brine overnight. Drain and rinse in cold water. Put the rind into the preserving pan with the water, bring to the boil and simmer for 20 minutes or until tender. Drain and reserve the liquid.

Put the reserved liquid back into the preserving pan with the sugar, vinegar, and spices tied in a muslin (cheesecloth) bag. Bring to the boil, stirring to dissolve the sugar, then add the rind and simmer until it becomes transparent. Remove the spices, then use a slotted spoon to transfer the rind to jars. Cover with the syrup, and seal. Store for at least 4 weeks before using.

Makes about 3 kg (6 lb)

———— ◆ ————

Watermelon contains about 91% water and
is an ideal fruit for slimmers.

Pickled Eggs

One of the mainstays of the English pub lunch, and one of the most useful pickles to have on hand—great for picnics or quick lunch snacks.

12 eggs
4½ cups (36 fl oz)
malt vinegar

1 teaspoon black
peppercorns
Dried chillies (see p. 2)

Hardboil the eggs, stirring occasionally to centre the yolk. Peel carefully. Bring the vinegar to the boil with the peppercorns. Allow to cool.

Pack the eggs into jars, cover with the strained vinegar and place a chilli or two in each jar. Seal and store for at least 3 weeks before opening. White wine vinegar can be used for a milder flavour, but malt vinegar is traditional.

Pickled Quail Eggs

These delicate little eggs need different treatment to the more robust hen eggs.

24 quail eggs
2½ cups (20 fl oz)
white wine vinegar
2 dried bay leaves
1 teaspoon black
peppercorns

2 teaspoons chopped
fresh ginger
(ginger root)

Simmer the quail eggs for 3 minutes. Put in cold water to cool, then shell. Boil the vinegar and spices for 5 minutes, then cool. Pack the eggs in a jar and cover with the strained vinegar. Seal and keep in the refrigerator. Eat the eggs within 3 weeks.

Pickled Jerusalem Artichokes

Here's one way of dealing with a glut of Jerusalem artichokes. Serve them with smoked chicken or smoked fish, or toss into a winter salad.

1 kg (2 lb) Jerusalem
    artichokes
Salt
5 cups (40 fl oz)
    white wine vinegar
4 bay leaves

2.5 cm (1 inch) piece
    of fresh ginger
    (ginger root), finely
    chopped (minced)
Peel of two lemons,
    finely chopped
    (minced)

Peel the artichokes and put them into salted water to prevent discolouration. Put the whole artichokes into boiling salted water and simmer for about 10 minutes or until just tender. Put the vinegar and other ingredients into a saucepan, bring to the boil and simmer for 10 minutes, then cool. Drain the artichokes and pack into jars. Cover with the cooled vinegar, distributing the bay leaves, ginger and lemon peel as evenly as possible. Keep for 2 weeks before using.

Makes about 2 kg (4 lb)

Pickled Asparagus

Nothing looks prettier on a buffet table than a platter of pickled asparagus and smoked salmon. But you should explain what it is to guests who may mistake it for commercially canned (it is a similar colour) and ignore it! The vinegar solution is diluted with white wine for a delicate flavour.

About 40 fresh
    asparagus spears
Water and salt
3 cups (24 fl oz)
    white wine vinegar

3 teaspoons finely
    chopped (minced)
    fresh ginger
    (ginger root)

3 cups (24 fl oz)
white wine
2 teaspoons black
peppercorns

1 blade of mace (if
unavailable 1
teaspoon ground
mace—see p. 16)

Break off the coarse ends of the asparagus, then trim with a knife so that the spears are an even length. Soak in salted water for 30 minutes. Meanwhile, bring the vinegar, wine and spices to the boil, simmer for 5 minutes and cool.

Bring some water to the boil in a pan, then lay the asparagus flat in the water. Simmer for 5 minutes, then remove from the pan and spread out on a board to cool as quickly as possible. Stand the asparagus in jars, packing the spears fairly tightly. Cover with vinegar and seal. Ready after a day and should be used within 3 weeks.

Makes about 2½ kg (5 lb)

Beetroot (Beet) Pickle

6 beetroots (beets)
1½ cups (12 fl oz) red
   wine vinegar
3 teaspoons mustard
   powder

1 teaspoon salt
1 cup (8 oz) sugar
3 teaspoons dill seeds

Cook the beetroots, with some stalk intact, for 15-20 minutes or until they are tender. Drain, setting aside 1½ cups (12 fl oz) of the cooking liquid. When the beetroots are cool, cut off the stalks and bottoms, then peel. Slice, then pack into warm, dry jars.

Bring the vinegar and reserved cooking liquid to the boil, add the mustard, salt and sugar. Stir to dissolve the sugar and simmer for about 5 minutes. Add the dill seeds to the jars with the beetroot, then cover completely with the hot vinegar mixture. Seal and when cool, store in the fridge. Leave for a few days before using. (Small whole beetroot can be pickled in the same way.)

Makes about 1½ kg (3 lb)

Pickled Red Cabbage

1 red cabbage
Approximately ½ cup
   (4 oz) salt
2 teaspoons mustard
   seeds
2 teaspoons caraway
   seeds
1 teaspoon black
   peppercorns
2 teaspoons allspice
   berries (Jamaican
   peppers)

2 teaspoons crushed
   fresh ginger
   (ginger root)
3 blades mace (if
   unavailable 3
   teaspoons ground
   mace—see p. 16)
4 cups (32 fl oz)
   white vinegar

Remove the outer leaves and hard central core from the cabbage, then shred finely across the grain. Place layers of shredded cabbage, sprinkled with salt, in a bowl. Cover and leave for 24 hours in a cool place, drain.

Put the spices and vinegar into a saucepan. Bring to the boil, simmer for 5 minutes, then remove from the heat and stand for 2 hours. Strain off the spices. Pack the cabbage in warm, dry jars and pour the vinegar over, making sure it is completely covered. Seal. Keep for 1 week before using and use within 4 months—otherwise the cabbage will lose its crispness.

Makes about 1½ kg (3 lb)

Pickled Celery

A lovely light pickle that goes well with delicately flavoured meat, such as poached chicken.

1 head celery
2 cups (16 fl oz) cider
*   vinegar*
2 teaspoons salt
2.5 cm (1 inch) piece
*   of fresh ginger*
*   (ginger root),*
*   peeled and sliced*

4 blades mace (if
*   unavailable 4*
*   teaspoons ground*
*   mace—see p. 16)*

Cut tops off the celery, wash the sticks well, wipe dry and cut to fit your jars. Put the vinegar, salt, ginger and mace into a saucepan, bring to the boil and simmer for 10 minutes. Add the celery, and when it returns to the boil, strain off the vinegar, discard the spices and put the celery in jars. Cool the vinegar and pour it over the celery. Seal and store for 1 week—use within 3 weeks.

Makes about 1½ kg (3 lb)

Pickled Capsicums (Peppers)

There are many variations on this versatile pickle. In this one, the skin is removed from the capsicums, subtly changing the flavour.

*6 capsicums (bell or
sweet peppers),
seeded and halved
lengthways
4½ cups (36 fl oz)
white wine vinegar*

*1 teaspoon salt
1 teaspoon black
peppercorns
Olive oil*

Place the capsicums, skin side up, under a hot grill (broiler) until the skin is black and charred. Rub off the charred skin. Cut the capsicums into broad slices and pack into warm, dry jars.

Bring the vinegar, salt and peppercorns to the boil and pour over the capsicums to cover completely. When cool, pour a layer of olive oil into the top of each jar. Seal and store.

Makes about 2 kg (4 lb)

Sweet Capsicum (Pepper) Pickle

*4 capsicums (bell or
sweet peppers),
seeded and cut into
broad strips
Dried oregano (wild
marjoram)
Dried red chillies*

*2 cups (16 fl oz)
white wine vinegar
3 cups (24 fl oz)
white wine
3 teaspoons salt
30 ml (1 fl oz) olive
oil*

Pack capsicums into jars with a sprinkling of oregano and some chillies (about 2 per jar). Heat the vinegar, wine and salt, and simmer for about 5 minutes. Cool, then pour over the capsicums. Pour a layer of olive oil on top. It will keep this way for about 2 months.

Makes about 2 kg (4 lb)

Moroccan Capsicums (Peppers)

This dish adds colour and flavour to an antipasto platter, but is also incredibly good served simply with crusty bread to soak up the oil.

> 2 large capsicums
> (bell or sweet
> peppers), seeded and
> cut into strips—you
> can use any colour,
> but don't mix
> colours in the one
> batch
>
> 6 cloves garlic
> 1 teaspoon salt
> ½ teaspoon cayenne
> pepper
> 1 cup (8 fl oz) olive
> oil
> ¾ cup (2 fl oz) white
> wine vinegar

Cook all the ingredients in an uncovered saucepan over low heat for about 30 minutes, stirring occasionally. Spoon into a jar. It will keep well in the refrigerator for about 3 weeks. Serve at room temperature.

Makes about 1 kg (2 lb)

Dilled Carrot Pickle

> 1 kg (2 lb) carrots,
> cut into straws
> (julienne-style)
> About 8 sprigs dill
> 3 teaspoons salt
>
> 1 cup (8 fl oz) cider
> vinegar
> 2 cups (16 fl oz)
> water

Blanch the carrots and put into jars with about 4 sprigs of dill to a jar. Bring the remaining ingredients to the boil and pour over the carrots and dill, making sure they are completely covered. Seal, and keep for 2 weeks before using.

Makes about 1½ kg (3 lb)

Pickled Julienne of Carrots and Celery

A decorative garnish to have on hand as well as a delicious vegetable accompaniment to grilled (broiled) chicken.

½ head of celery
4 carrots
Salted water
4 cups (32 fl oz)
  white wine vinegar

1 cup (8 oz) sugar
6 star anise
½ cup (4 fl oz) soy
  sauce

Cut the vegetables into thin julienne strips and leave to stand in a bowl of salted water while you prepare the spiced vinegar. Bring the vinegar to the boil with the sugar, star anise and soy sauce. Drain the vegetables, then pack into jars. Cover with hot liquid, then seal when cool. Leave for at least 1 week before using.

Pickled Eggplants (Aubergines)

A delicious accompaniment to lamb kebabs (shish kabob), but also good with cold lamb.

1 kg (2 lb) small
  eggplants
  (aubergines), sliced
2 tablespoons salt
2½ cups (20 fl oz) red
  wine vinegar
4 cloves garlic,
  chopped

2 teaspoons dried
  sweet marjoram
2 teaspoons dried
  basil
Olive oil

Put the eggplants into a colander and sprinkle each layer with salt. Put a plate on top and leave for 2 hours. Press to remove excess moisture, then drain. Bring the vinegar to the boil, add the eggplant and simmer for 5 minutes. Strain the eggplant and layer in jars with the garlic, marjoram and basil. Cool the vinegar, then pour it over the eggplants. Top with a layer of olive oil. Seal and keep for at least 2 weeks before opening.

Makes about 1½ kg (3 lb)

Pickled Horseradish

2 cups water
6 teaspoons sugar
3 teaspoons salt

2 cups horseradish,
  grated (shredded)
  (it's a good idea
  to do this in the
  open air)

Heat the water, sugar and salt, stirring to dissolve. Cool and mix with the grated horseradish. Pour into jars and seal. Store in the refrigerator.

Makes about 500 g (1 lb)

Mushrooms in Brine

1 kg (2 lb) whole	*5 cups (40 fl oz)*
button mushrooms	*water*
200 g (8 oz) salt	*3 teaspoons black*
¼ cup (2 oz) sugar	*peppercorns*

Wipe the mushrooms with a damp cloth to clean, then pack into warm, dry jars. Bring the other ingredients to the boil and simmer for 5 minutes. Strain the hot liquid into jars to completely cover the mushrooms. Seal and store for up to 6 months.

Makes about 1 kg (2 lb)

Mushrooms Pickled in Oil

Serve these mushrooms as an hors d'oeuvre with drinks—also delicious with steak and hamburgers.

1 kg (2 lb) whole	*1 cup (8 fl oz) olive oil*
button mushrooms	*¾ cup (6 fl oz) red*
1 teaspoon salt	*wine vinegar*
6 teaspoons finely	*3 cloves garlic, finely*
chopped (minced)	*chopped (minced)*
parsley	*Black pepper*

Wash the mushrooms and put into a saucepan with salt. Cover and cook in their own liquid for about 10 minutes, stirring occasionally. Add the parsley in the last minute of cooking. Mix the oil, vinegar and garlic with black pepper to taste. Drain the mushrooms, put into warm, dry jars, cover with the oil mixture and seal. Can be used after a few days. Store in a cool place.

NOTE: *If you plan to keep the mushrooms for longer than a couple of weeks, substitute safflower oil (or another polyunsaturated oil) for olive oil and keep in the fridge.*

Makes about 1 kg (2 lb)

Pickled Okra (Ladies Fingers)

Great with Greek lamb casseroles.

1 kg (2 lb) okra
(ladies fingers),
trimmed at stalk end
2 fresh chillies per
jar (see p. 2)
1 clove garlic per jar
4½ cups (36 fl oz)
white wine vinegar

2 teaspoons mustard
seeds
1 teaspoon black
peppercorns
50 g (2 oz salt)

Wash the okra, then cook in boiling salted water for 3 minutes. Drain, then spread on a board to cool. Pack into jars and add 2 chillies and 1 clove of garlic to each. Bring the vinegar and spices to the boil and simmer for 5 minutes. Cool, then strain and pour over the okra. Seal and store for 2 months before opening.

Makes about 2 kg (4 lb)

Crisp Okra (Ladies Fingers) Pickle

½ kg (1 lb) okra
(ladies fingers),
trimmed at stem end
1 fresh chilli per jar
(see p. 2)
1 clove garlic per jar

4 cups (32 fl oz)
white wine vinegar
½ cup (4 fl oz) water
6 teaspoons salt
3 teaspoons mustard
seeds, black or white

Wash the okra, blanch (bring some water to the boil in a saucepan, add the okra, and when water returns to the boil, drain) and pack into jars. Add 1 fresh chilli and 1 clove of garlic to each jar. Combine the vinegar with the remaining ingredients in a saucepan. Bring to the boil and simmer for a few minutes. Pour over the okra, covering completely. Use after 2 weeks.

Makes about 1 kg (2 lb)

Spiced Rhubarb

Spiced fruits are versatile—this one goes as well with roast lamb or pork as it does with ice-cream!

¾ cup (6 fl oz) malt
    vinegar
¾ cup (6 fl oz) water
1 teaspoon allspice
    berries (Jamaican
    peppers)
½ teaspoon nutmeg
4 cloves

½ teaspoon
    cinnamon
4 cups (2 lb) sugar
1½ kg (3 lb) rhubarb,
    washed, trimmed
    and cut into 2.5 cm
    (1 inch) pieces

Heat the vinegar, water, spices, and sugar in a saucepan, stirring to dissolve the sugar. Simmer for 15 minutes. Strain off the whole spices and return the syrup to the saucepan. Add the rhubarb and cook gently, uncovered, until the mixture is thick. Pour into jars and seal.

Makes about 2 kg (4 lb)

Zucchini (Courgette) Pickles

1 kg (2 lb) zucchini
    (courgettes),
    thinly sliced
1 onion, thinly sliced
50 g (2 oz) salt
2 cups (16 fl oz)
    white wine vinegar

1 cup (8 oz) sugar
1 teaspoon celery
    seeds
1 teaspoon anise
    seeds
1 teaspoon white
    mustard seeds

Layer the zucchini and onion in a bowl, sprinkling with salt. Leave for 2 hours, then rinse in cold water and drain well. Combine the vinegar, sugar, and celery, anise and mustard seeds in a saucepan. Bring to the boil and simmer for a few minutes. Remove from the heat, add the zucchini and onions, and leave for 1 hour. Bring the mixture back to the boil, then remove from the heat and ladle into jars. Seal when cool.

Makes about 1½ kg (3 lb)

Here are two other versions of spiced vinegar, using a slightly different method to that described at p. 16 in the introduction. Adjust the spices as you like.

Mild Spiced Vinegar 2

4½ cups (36 fl oz)
vinegar—must be at
least 5 per cent
acetic acid to act
as a preservative
1 cinnamon stick
10 cloves
4 blades mace (if
unavailable omit)

12 allspice berries
(Jamaican peppers)
8 black peppercorns
(Additional
flavourings, such
as coriander seeds
and bay leaves,
can be added)

Warm the vinegar, but don't boil, then add the spices and allow to steep for at least 2 hours. Strain and use as required.

Hot Spiced Vinegar 2

4½ cups (36 fl oz)
vinegar—must be
at least 5 per cent
acetic acid to act
as a preservative
25 g (1 oz) mustard
seeds, white or
black
24 cloves
24 black peppercorns
25 g (1 oz) allspice
berries (Jamaican
peppers)

25 g (1 oz) whole
dried chillies
(see p. 2)
(Additional
flavourings, such
as crushed fresh
ginger (ginger
root) and scraped
horseradish, can
be added)

Method as above.

Pickled Vegetables

The spiced vinegars in this book can be used to pickle almost any vegetable; zucchini (courgettes), chokos (christophene, chayote), onions, carrots, beans, cauliflower, celery, radish, cucumbers, cabbage and many others are suitable.

To prepare the vegetable of your choice or a combination: cut the carrots and zucchini into rounds or straws (julienne-style), dice the larger vegetables or cut into straws, peel the small onions and leave whole, leave the beans whole or cut into strips, leave small vegetables whole, cut cauliflower into florets.

Place the vegetables in a bowl. They can then be sprinkled with layers of cooking salt (about 1 tablespoon of salt to each 500 g [1 lb] vegetables) or covered with a brine.

* To make the brine: dissolve ¾ cup (8 oz) salt in every 10 cups (80 fl oz) boiling water. Cool before using. It's important that vegetables are completely covered by the solution—a plate and a small weight can be used to hold them under.

Brine is used for most vegetables, but dry salting is best for vegetables, such as zucchini and cucumber, with a high water content.

Leave the vegetables in salt or brine for one to two days, then rinse in clean, cold water and drain well before packing into jars and covering with spiced vinegar.

Vinegar is usually used cold with vegetables to keep them crisp, while hot vinegar gives a good result with softer fruit pickles.

———— ◆ ————

Vinegar has been used both as a disinfectant and antidote to infection, and as a beauty aid to freshen and whiten the complexion. The ancient Egyptians used vinegar not only as a seasoning for foodstuffs but also as a medicine for fevers.

ASIAN PICKLES

Acar (Cucumber Pickles)

Serve with Indonesian or Thai food.

2 cups (16 fl oz) water	½ kg (1 lb) cucumbers, cut into thick slices
2 cups (16 fl oz) white wine vinegar	1 red capsicum (bell or sweet pepper),
⅓ cup (2½ oz) sugar	seeded and diced
Salt	1 red (Italian) onion,
4 dried chillies (see p. 2)	thinly sliced
2 cloves garlic, peeled	
3 teaspoons finely chopped (minced) fresh ginger (ginger root)	

Combine the water, vinegar, sugar, salt, dried chillies, garlic and ginger in a saucepan. Bring to the boil and simmer for 10 minutes. Mix the cucumbers, capsicum and red onion in a bowl with a tight-fitting lid. Pour over the hot vinegar and cover when cool. Store in the fridge. This pickle should be eaten within 1 week, but should be made at least 1 day in advance.

Makes about 1 kg (2 lb)

Japanese Salt Pickle

Pickles are an important part of any Japanese meal. Serve this unusual pickle as a side dish with soy sauce or Japanese rice wine vinegar.

2 cucumbers or 2 large white radishes (daikon)—don't mix in the one batch	4 fresh chillies, seeded and cut into strips (see p. 2)

6 teaspoons salt (use
more if necessary)

Peel and seed the cucumbers and cut into 1 cm (½ inch) slices. If using white radishes, peel and halve vertically, then cut into slices. Dry the vegetables, then layer in a glass or ceramic bowl with sprinklings of salt, starting and ending with layers of salt. Slip the chillies into the bowl. Cover with a plate that fits inside the bowl, and place a weight on top. Store in the fridge. After about 4 days they will be ready, but they will keep for more than 1 month. To eat, lift out some pickle, drain, then rinse in cold water and dry.

Makes about 500 g (1 lb)

Japanese Pickled Eggplant

This recipe can be made on the day or a few days ahead.

500 g (1 lb) small
eggplants
(aubergines)
Salt
2 teaspoons Japanese
horseradish (wasabi)
powder or English
mustard powder

45 ml (1½ fl oz)
Japanese rice
wine vinegar
3 teaspoons sugar
45 ml (1½ fl oz) soy
sauce

Wash and cut the eggplants into thick slices. Put in a colander and sprinkle with salt. Leave for 1 hour. Drain, rinse in cold water, dry and put into a glass or ceramic bowl. Mix the horseradish powder with water to make a paste, then add the Japanese rice wine vinegar, sugar and soy sauce. Add to the eggplant slices, tossing gently so they are covered with the mixture. Cover and keep in the fridge for at least 3 hours, turning occasionally.

Makes about 500 g (1 lb)

Pickled Ginger

This pickle which is both sharp and sweet is a traditional accompaniment to sushi.

100 g (4 oz) fresh
   ginger (ginger
   root)
salt

½ cup (4 fl oz) rice
   wine vinegar
3 teaspoons sugar

Peel the ginger and carefully cut into the thinnest possible slices. Put into a bowl, cover with water and leave for about 30 minutes. Drain, then blanch, and put into a jar. Sprinkle with a little salt. Heat the vinegar and sugar, stirring to dissolve, then pour over the ginger. When cool, seal and store in the fridge. Ready to use after 1 week but will keep for several months.

Makes about 1 cup (8 oz)

Pickled Garlic

2 heads garlic
½ cup (4 fl oz) cider
   vinegar

½ cup (4 fl oz) soy
   sauce
6 teaspoons sugar

Peel the cloves of garlic and put them into a jar. Bring the other ingredients to the boil and simmer until slightly reduced. Pour the hot liquid over the garlic. Allow to cool before sealing. Keep for 3 weeks before using.

Makes about 2 cups (16 fl oz)

—— ◆ ——

*The juice of garlic is a powerful antiseptic
and was widely used during both
World Wars.*

Seafood (and meat) can also be pickled: here are two simple recipes.

NOTE: *Neither is long lasting.*

Gravlax

Marinated salmon is a Scandinavian speciality—traditionally the fish was packed in snow during the curing process. Its perfect partners are Dill Mustard Dressing (see page 9) and rye bread.

1 kg (2 lb) fillets	3 teaspoons crushed
· fresh salmon or	white peppercorns
salmon trout	1 bunch fresh dill
½ cup (4 oz) sugar	½ cup (4 fl oz) white
½ cup (4 oz) coarse	wine
salt	½ cup (4 fl oz) brandy

Select a glass or ceramic dish just large enough to hold the fish. Place one fillet in the dish, skin side down. Sprinkle with a mixture of sugar, salt, peppercorns and a few sprigs of dill. Cover with a second fillet, skin side up. Sandwich the remaining fillets in this way.

Combine the white wine and brandy and pour into the dish, then cover with plastic wrap and a weight (for instance, a large bottle of soft drink, or a couple of cans). Keep in the fridge for 3 days, taking out twice a day to turn the fish, and thoroughly baste with the marinade.

To serve, transfer the fish to a chopping board, separate the fillets and scrape off the dill and seasonings. Slice the fish horizontally, leaving the skin on. Will keep for 1 week.

Makes about 1 kg (2 lb)

Ceviche of Scallops

Pickled raw fish is popular in the South Pacific: the fish is 'cooked' in lemon juice (or lime juice) and the flesh becomes opaque. It should be eaten the day it's made.

500 g (1 lb) scallops
Juice of 2 lemons (or
3 limes)
2 sticks celery, diced
1 small red (Italian)
onion, finely sliced
Finely chopped
(minced) parsley

1 clove garlic, finely
chopped
30 ml (1 fl oz) olive
oil
Salt and black
pepper
Lemon wedges

Remove any brown or black bits from the scallops and place in a glass or ceramic bowl with the lemon or lime juice. Leave in the fridge for 3 hours. Drain off the lemon juice. Toss the celery and onion through the scallops. Mix the parsley, garlic and olive oil with salt and black pepper, and pour it over the scallops. Mix and return to the fridge for another hour or so before serving. Serve with lemon wedges.

CHUTNEYS, RELISHES AND SAUCES

It is impossible to have a failure with chutney; there's nothing to set and no ingredient barred.

Robert Morley

The name chutney comes from the Hindu word *chatni* and stems from its finger-licking qualities when fingers were the favoured eating utensil! The British raj took to these spicy condiments with enthusiasm and in the 19th century most English cook books included a wide range of recipes for chutneys as well as pickles. But while English chutneys make an excellent accompaniment to Indian food, they are quite different to chutneys prepared by Indian cooks. The British adapted Indian recipes and it's their adaptations that have become accepted as traditional: strong, sweet relishes with a unique taste that depends on long slow cooking, then storing for a long time for the flavour to mature. Fruit and/or vegetables are chopped finely (minced), cooked until they form a thick smooth mass (usually with none of the individual ingredients recognisable) and preserved with vinegar, sugar, salt and spices.

But Indian cooks often prepare chutney with raw fruit and vegetables a short time before they are eaten. Now, once again we're following their lead and this sort of instant chutney is becoming popular in the West.

Instant chutneys require top quality ingredients, but this isn't so important with long-maturing chutneys, as long as any bruised or damaged parts are cut out. Dried fruits can also be used, and sometimes canned or frozen fruit and vegetables, so that you can make almost any type of traditional chutney at any time of the year.

Malt vinegar is most often used in chutneys, but white vinegar can be used if a lighter colour and less intense flavour is desired. You will need less vinegar if you add it gradually as cooking proceeds.

Ground spices are normally used but if you prefer the flavour of whole spices, they can be tied in a muslin (cheesecloth) bag, added to the mixture, then removed before pouring into jars.

Either white or brown sugar can be used depending on whether a dark or a lighter chutney is required. (Except when otherwise specified, the sugar in recipes refers to white granular sugar.) It's a good idea, but not absolutely necessary, to warm the sugar before adding it to the chutney so it dissolves more quickly. To warm the sugar, spread it in a shallow baking dish and put into a slow oven for about 10 minutes, stirring occasionally to distribute the heat.

Chutneys are, unless stated otherwise, cooked without a lid and stirred frequently. To test that it is ready, draw a wooden spoon across the bottom of the pan. If it leaves a clean line the chutney is ready to bottle. Allow the chutney to cool very slightly in the pan before pouring it into jars.

Relishes are similar to chutneys, but the cooking time is not as long and the finished preserve contains recognisable pieces of vegetable and/or fruit.

Sauces and ketchups are made in a similar way to chutney, then sieved to give a sauce consistency.

Essential equipment for making all of these is a large preserving pan, preferably made of stainless steel or aluminium. Brass, copper or iron pans should not be used as they react with the vinegar and give a metallic flavour. The pan should be big enough to hold large quantites of ingredients and should be wide enough in diameter to allow for the evaporation that is an essential part of the thickening process.

You will also need a long-handled wooden spoon; it's a good idea to keep one exclusively for chutney making as the spices will impregnate the wood and could affect other foods. A ladle and a heat-proof jug are necessary aids to filling jars. A funnel can also be a help pouring sauces into bottles.

Jars should be thoroughly washed, then dried and warmed in a slow oven. Put the wet jars into the oven (not touching each other) before turning it on to the lowest temperature. Pour the hot chutney into warm, dry jars. Covers must be air-tight.

Use jars with clip-on glass lids or plastic screw-tops. Paraffin wax (available at pharmacies and supermarkets (US)) can also be used: melt over a low heat (do not heat more than is necessary to melt) and pour a thin layer on to the surface of the chutney—when almost set, pour on another layer and insert a piece of string to make it easier to remove. Metal lids must not be used (vinegar will corrode the metal and make the chutney inedible) unless lined with plastic. Do not use paper or jam covers as the vinegar will evaporate and the chutney will shrink and dry out.

Finished preserves should be labelled with the name and date of making, then stored in a cool, dark, dry place.

Chutneys need at least 2 months to mature. Most will keep well for at least 2 years—and some will keep for 20 years!

Apple and Pineapple Chutney

1 kg (2 lb) cooking apples, peeled, cored and chopped
1 cup (8 fl oz) water
1 cup (½ lb) brown sugar

1 teaspoon ground cinnamon
1 teaspoon ground cloves
½ cup (4 oz) sultanas (golden raisins)

1 pineapple, peeled,
  cored and chopped
1 teaspoon salt
3 teaspoons chopped
  preserved ginger

1 cup (8 fl oz) malt
  vinegar

Simmer the apples, water and sugar for 15 minutes before adding all other ingredients except the vinegar. Stir well. Simmer for another 15 minutes, then add the vinegar. Simmer until thick, stirring occasionally. Pour into jars and seal.

Makes about 2 kg (4 lb)

Pressure Cooker (Canner) Apple Chutney

If you have a pressure cooker it will save fuel when making chutney.

1½ kg (3 lb) cooking
  apples
100 g (4 oz) chopped
  walnuts
300 g (12 oz) seedless
  dark raisins
½ teaspoon ground
  cloves

½ cup (4 fl oz) white
  vinegar
4 cups (2 lb) sugar
Grated rind of 1
  orange

Peel and core the apples, then slice. Place in a pressure cooker with the other ingredients and cook for 15 minutes. When the pressure drops, remove the lid. If the chutney is not thick enough, continue cooking for a short time without the lid to evaporate excess liquid.

Makes about 2 kg (4 lb)

Bengal Chutney

A favourite in the days of the Raj.

1½ kg (3 lb) cooking
  apples, cored and
  quartered
100 g (4 oz) seedless
  dark raisins
2 cloves garlic
½ cup (4 oz) sugar
3 teaspoons ground
  ginger

1 teaspoon cayenne
  pepper
1 teaspoon white
  mustard seeds
Juice and grated rind
  of 1 lemon
4 cups (32 fl oz)
  white vinegar

Mince the apples, raisins and garlic in a food processor, then combine with the other ingredients in a preserving pan. Bring to the boil, and simmer for 2 hours or until thickened, stirring occasionally. Pour into jars and seal.

Makes about 1½ kg (3 lb)

Dried Apricot and Apple Chutney

This is a quick maturing chutney that you can eat after a couple of weeks.

500 g (1 lb) dried apricots
250 g (½ lb) dried apples
2 cloves garlic
Juice and rind of 1 lemon
1 teaspoon salt
2 teaspoons allspice berries (Jamaican peppers) in a muslin (cheesecloth) bag

1 teaspoon mustard powder
2½ cups (20 fl oz) malt vinegar
2 cups (1 lb) dark brown sugar

Chop the apricots and apples, and soak overnight in water. Next day, drain and put into a pan with all the other ingredients except the sugar. Cook for about 30 minutes then add the sugar, stir well, and bring the chutney slowly to the boil. Simmer until the chutney has thickened—about 20 minutes. Remove the allspice, pour into jars and seal.

Makes about 1 kg (2 lb)

———— ◆ ————

Apricots originated in China where they have been grown for 4000 years. Fresh apricots are a good source of Vitamin A, while dried apricots are an excellent source of iron.

Dried Apricot Chutney

Dried apricots work as well as fresh in chutney.

500 g (1 lb) dried
apricots
2½ cups (20 fl oz)
malt vinegar
1 fresh chilli, seeded
and finely chopped
(minced) (see p. 2)
1 cinnamon stick
1 cup (½ lb) soft
brown sugar
1 teaspoon white
pepper

1 teaspoon mustard
seeds
1 teaspoon ground
allspice (Jamaican
peppers)
2 teaspoons finely
chopped minced
fresh ginger
(ginger root)

Soak the apricots in water for about 1 hour. Bring the vinegar to the boil with all the other ingredients except the apricots. Simmer for 15 minutes, then add the apricots. Cook for 20 minutes more or until the mixture thickens. Pour into jars and seal while hot. Keep for at least 3 weeks before using.

Makes about 750 g (1½ lb)

Cherry Chutney (1)

The only draw-back to this recipe is pitting the cherries, but you can buy gadgets that help.

1 kg (2 lbs) cherries,
pitted and chopped
1 cup (6 oz) currants
(dried)
½ cup (4 oz) sugar

30 ml (1 fl oz)
molasses
1 cup (8 fl oz) red
wine vinegar

Put all the ingredients into a preserving pan and bring to the boil, stirring to dissolve the sugar. Simmer for about 30 minutes, stirring frequently, until thick. Spoon into jars and seal.

Makes about 1 kg (2 lb)

Cherry Chutney (2)

1 kg (2 lb) cherries, pitted	2 fresh chillies, seeded and finely
1 cup (8 fl oz) red wine vinegar	chopped (minced) (see p. 2)
1 cup (8 fl oz) brown sugar	1 teaspoon ground cinnamon
2 bay leaves	1 teaspoon salt
1 teaspoon ground cloves	1 teaspoon pepper

Put all the ingredients into a preserving pan and cook with the lid on for 30 minutes over low heat, stirring occasionally. Remove the lid and continue to cook, stirring constantly, for 30 minutes or until thick and pulpy. If the liquid evaporates too quickly add a little more vinegar. Pour into jars and seal.

Makes about 1 kg (2 lb)

Banana Chutney

1 kg (2 lb) bananas, sliced	100 g (4 oz) preserved ginger, finely
1 kg (2 lb) apples, peeled, cored and diced	chopped (minced)
500 g (1 lb) onions, finely chopped (minced)	2 fresh chillies, seeded and finely chopped (see p. 2)
500 g (1 lb) seedless dark raisins	3 teaspoons salt
	5 cups (40 fl oz) vinegar
	2 cups (1 lb) sugar

Put all the ingredients, except the sugar, into a preserving pan and bring to the boil. Add the sugar and stir to dissolve. Simmer for 2 hours or until thick. Pour into jars and seal.

Makes about 2½ kg (5 lb)

Cranberry Relish

Delicious with baked ham and turkey.

1 kg (2 lb)	*2 cups (1 lb) sugar*
cranberries, picked	*1 cup (8 fl oz) orange*
over	*juice*
2 thin-skinned navel	
oranges	

Roughly process the cranberries in a food processor and scrape into a bowl. Roughly chop and seed the oranges, and put into the food processor (including the rind) with the sugar and orange juice. Process until finely chopped (minced). Pour into the bowl with the cranberries and combine. Leave in the refrigerator overnight—it will keep for a few days. Stir again before serving.

Makes about 2 kg (4 lb)

Cranberry Sauce

This recipe can be used for other berries—fresh or frozen.

1 kg (2 lb) cranberries, picked over	2 cups water 1½ cups (12 oz) sugar

Put the cranberries into a heavy saucepan, add the water, bring to the boil and simmer, covered, for 10 minutes. Add the sugar and stir until dissolved, then simmer with the lid on for 15 minutes, stirring occasionally. Will keep in the refrigerator for up to 1 week. Serve at room temperature.

Makes about 1 kg (2 lb)

Cumberland Sauce

A lovely fruity sauce that is always served cold—excellent with baked ham, pickled pork, or game, also brawn and terrines.

¹/₃ cup (2½ oz) redcurrant jelly 30 ml (1 fl oz) lemon juice 2 tablespoons orange marmalade	¼ cup (2 fl oz) port wine 3 teaspoons Dijon mustard

Mix all ingredients together thoroughly. Spoon into a jar. It keeps well in the fridge.

———— ◆ ————

*The currant was first cultivated
sometime before 1600 in the Netherlands,
Denmark and around the Baltic Sea. There are
also many varieties native to North America.*

Date and Banana Chutney

6 bananas, thinly
sliced
225 g (8 oz) stoned
dates, chopped
225 g (8 oz) cooking
apples, peeled and
chopped
4 onions, chopped
1½ cups (12 fl oz)
malt vinegar

½ cup (4 oz)
crystallised (candied)
ginger, chopped
1 teaspoon salt
1 teaspoon ground
allspice (Jamaican
pepper)
2 teaspoons curry
powder (see p. 2)
1 cup (8 fl oz) molasses

Put the bananas, dates, apples and onions into a preserving pan with
the vinegar. Cook slowly, until soft, then mash the mixture to a pulp
with a wooden spoon. Add the crystallised ginger, salt and spices.
Continue to cook slowly until the chutney looks thick and pulpy, then
stir in the molasses. If the mixture is too sticky, add a little more vinegar.
Cook for 15-20 minutes, stirring occasionally, until the mixture is thick
and a rich brown colour. Pour into jars and seal.

Makes about 1½ kg (3 lb)

Fig and Ginger Chutney

1 kg (2 lb) fresh figs
1 onion, finely
chopped (minced)
2 cups (16 fl oz) malt
vinegar
1½ cups (12 oz) sugar
½ cup (3 oz) chopped
preserved ginger

1½ cups (8 oz)
seedless dark
raisins
½ teaspoon each
mixed spice, curry
powder and
ground cinnamon
1 teaspoon salt

Wash the figs, remove the stems and chop into small pieces. Place in a pan with the onion and half the vinegar. Bring to the boil and simmer until pulpy. Add the remaining vinegar, and the sugar, ginger, raisins, spices and salt. Stir until boiling. Simmer uncovered, stirring occasionally, until thickened. Pour into jars and seal when cool.

Makes about 1 kg (2 lb)

NOTE: *You can buy ready-mixed spice, but to make mixed spice combine the following proportions of ground spices:*

1 teaspoon cinnamon	*¼ teaspoon nutmeg*
½ teaspoon ginger	*¼ teaspoon cloves*

Kiwi Fruit (Chinese Gooseberries) Chutney

12 kiwi fruit (Chinese gooseberries), peeled and finely chopped (minced)
3 onions, finely chopped (minced)
1 banana, sliced
2 lemons, pith removed, cut into chunks

100 g (4 oz) sultanas (golden raisins)
100 g (4 oz) preserved ginger, finely chopped (minced)
2 teaspoons salt
½ teaspoon white pepper
1 cup (8 fl oz) white vinegar
1 cup (8 oz) sugar

Put all ingredients, except the sugar, into a preserving pan, and bring to the boil. Simmer for 45 minutes. Add the sugar, stirring until it dissolves. Continue cooking, stirring occasionally, until thick. Pour into jars and seal.

Makes about 1½ kg (3 lb)

Honeydew Melon Chutney

1 honeydew melon	1 cinnamon stick
Brine—50 g (2 oz) salt dissolved in 2½ cups (20 fl oz) water	1 large onion, finely chopped (minced)
2 cups (16 fl oz) cider vinegar	1 capsicum (bell or sweet pepper) seeded and finely chopped (minced)
2 cups (1 lb) sugar	
½ teaspoon salt	1 clove garlic, finely chopped (minced)
1 teaspoon ground ginger	100 g (4 oz) dried currants
½ teaspoon cayenne pepper	½ cup (4 fl oz) brandy
1 teaspoon ground allspice (Jamaican pepper)	

Peel and seed the melon, then cut the flesh into 1 inch (2.5 cm) cubes. Put the cubes into a bowl of brine and leave in the fridge overnight. Drain the melon and rinse in cold water.

Put all ingredients, except the currants and brandy, into a preserving pan. Bring to the boil, stirring occasionally, then add the currants and brandy. Simmer for 2 hours or until thick, stirring frequently. Pour into jars and seal.

Makes about 1 kg (2 lb)

Mango and Date Chutney

Fruit juice is used as a sweetener in this recipe, but as it does not have the preservative qualities of sugar, it is not a long-lasting chutney.

1 cup (8 fl oz) orange juice	2 cloves garlic, finely chopped (minced)
1 cup (8 fl oz) apple cider vinegar	1 onion, finely chopped (minced)

500 g (1 lb) dates,
    seeded
1 kg (2 lb) mangoes,
    peeled and sliced
3 teaspoons finely
    chopped (minced)
    fresh ginger
    (ginger root)

½ teaspoon ground
    chillies (see p. 2)

Put the orange juice, vinegar and seeded dates into a food processor
and make a rough puree. Combine with all the other ingredients in
a preserving pan. Bring to the boil and simmer gently, stirring frequently,
for about 40 minutes or until thick. Pour into jars and seal. Store in
the refrigerator.

Makes about 1½ kg (3 lb)

Tinned Mango Chutney

Approximately 1 kg
    (2 lb) tinned
    mangoes
2 onions
½ cup (2 oz)
    crystallised ginger
½ cup (2 oz) sultanas
    (golden raisins)
1 cup (8 oz) soft
    brown sugar
2 teaspoons salt

½ teaspoon dry
    mustard
¼ teaspoon ground
    cloves
1 teaspoon ground
    ginger
½ teaspoon cayenne
    pepper
3 cups (24 fl oz) malt
    vinegar

Slice the mangoes into small pieces. Peel the onions and chop finely.
Place all the ingredients, including the mango syrup, in a pan. Bring
to the boil, stirring constantly. Simmer, uncovered, until thickened, about
2 hrs. Pour into jars and seal.

Makes about 1 kg (2 lb)

Mango Chutney ✓

6 large green
   mangoes, peeled
   and sliced
1½ cups (12 oz)
   light brown sugar
3 cloves garlic,
   chopped
1½ cups (12 fl oz)
   malt vinegar

10 dry chillies,
   crushed (see p. 2)
3 teaspoons finely
   chopped (minced)
   fresh ginger
   (ginger root)

add caraway seeds
black cardamom seeds

Combine all ingredients in a preserving pan, bring slowly to the boil and simmer, stirring occasionally, for 1-2 hours or until thick. Pour into jars and seal.

Makes about 1 kg (2 lb)

Lemon Chutney

3 lemons, chopped
  into small pieces
  with seeds removed
3 teaspoons salt
2 onions, finely
  chopped (minced)
1½ cups (12 fl oz)
  cider vinegar

1 teaspoon ground
  allspice (Jamaican
  pepper)
6 teaspoons white
  mustard seeds
1 cup (8 oz) sugar
50 g (2 oz) seedless
  dark raisins

Put the chopped lemons into a colander and sprinkle with salt. Cover and leave overnight. Next day, combine the salted lemons with the other ingredients in a preserving pan, and bring to the boil. Simmer for about 1 hour, or until the lemons are soft. Spoon the chutney into jars. Seal and store.

Makes about 500 g (1 lb)

Nectarine Chutney

In this unusual recipe, fruit juice is used as a sweetener instead of sugar.
The chutney must be kept in the fridge.

1 kg (2 lb) nectarines	*1 cup (8 fl oz) apple juice*
1 cup (8 oz) chopped	*1 cup (8 fl oz) apple*
dried figs	*cider vinegar*
1 onion, finely	*1 teaspoon ground*
chopped (minced)	*cinnamon*

Plunge the nectarines into boiling water, then peel, remove the stones
(pits) and chop. Put the nectarines into a preserving pan with all the
other ingredients and simmer for about 40 minutes, breaking up the
ingredients with a wooden spoon during cooking to give a smooth texture.
When it thickens, pour into jars and seal. Store in the refrigerator.

Makes about 1 kg (2 lb)

Orange Chutney

10 oranges	*2 teaspoons ground*
2 lemons	*ginger*
2 apples	*1 teaspoon chilli*
3 onions	*powder (see p. 2)*
100 g (4 oz) seedless	*3 cups (24 fl oz) malt*
dark raisins	*vinegar*
2 cups (1 lb) sugar	
1 teaspoon ground	
black pepper	

Grate the orange and lemon rinds, and put into a preserving pan. Remove
as much of the white pith as possible from the oranges and lemons,
cut the flesh into small pieces, removing the pips, and add to the pan.
Peel and finely chop the apples and onions, then add to the pan with
the remaining ingredients. Simmer for about 1 hour or until thickened.
Bottle and seal while hot.

Makes about 2 kg (4 lb)

Pressure Cooker (Canner) Orange Chutney

4 oranges	2 cups (16 fl oz) malt
1 lemon	vinegar
225 g (8 oz) dates,	½ teaspoon ground
stones (pits) removed	chillies (see p. 2)
100 g (4 oz) seedless	1 teaspoon salt
dark raisins	1½ cups (12 oz) sugar
2 onions, roughly	
chopped	

Thinly pare the rind from one of the oranges and the lemon, then cut the rind and all the pith from the oranges including the one without the rind, and the lemon. Cut the oranges and lemons into pieces, remove the seeds, then roughly puree in the food processor with the dates, raisins, orange and lemon rind, and onions—you will have to do this in a couple of stages.

Put these ingredients into a pressure cooker, add the vinegar, ground chillies and salt. Cover the cooker, bring it to high pressure and cook for 5 minutes. When the pressure drops, open the pressure cooker and add the sugar. Stir over low heat to dissolve the sugar, then bring the chutney to the boil and simmer, stirring frequently, uncovered, for 15 minutes or until it thickens. Pour the chutney into jars and cover when cool. Ready after about 6 weeks.

Makes about 1 kg (2 lb)

———— ◆ ————

*The Seville sour orange actually reached
Europe before the sweet orange. Apart
from its use in marmalades and chutney
the grated rind and juice can be used as a
flavouring. It is a native of tropical Asia.*

Pawpaw (Papaya) Chutney

1 kg (2 lb) pawpaw
(papaya), peeled,
seeded and chopped
1 clove garlic
1 teaspoon black
pepper
1 teaspoon ground
nutmeg
1 cup (8 oz) sultanas
(golden raisins)

3 teaspoons finely
chopped (minced)
fresh ginger
(ginger root)
3 onions, finely
chopped (minced)
2 cups (1 lb) brown
sugar
2½ cups (20 fl oz)
malt vinegar

Combine all ingredients in a preserving pan, bring slowly to the boil and simmer, stirring occasionally, for 1 hour or until thick. Pour into jars and seal.

Makes about 1½ kg (3 lb)

Plum Sauce

A very versatile sauce—excellent as a dip for meatballs or pork spareribs.

2 kg (4 lb) plums
2 onions
1 cup (4 oz) sultanas
 (golden raisins)
2 teaspoons each
 allspice (Jamaican
 pepper), peppercorns
 and mustard (black
 or white) seeds
½ teaspoon cayenne
 pepper

2.5 cm (1 inch) piece
 of fresh ginger
 (ginger root), crushed
2½ cups (20 fl oz)
 malt vinegar
1 heaped teaspoon
 salt
1 cup (8 oz) soft
 brown sugar

Wash the plums and chop them. Peel and chop the onions. Put the plums and onions into a pan with the sultanas, spices and half the vinegar. Bring to the boil, then simmer gently for 30 minutes, or until the plums are soft and pulpy. Rub the mixture through a sieve then return the sauce to the pan. Add the remaining vinegar, salt and sugar. Bring to the boil, stirring until the sugar has dissolved. Simmer uncovered, stirring occasionally, for about 1 hour or until the sauce starts to thicken. Pour into bottles and seal at once.

Makes about 2 kg (4 lb)

NOTE: *Add some fresh seeded and chopped chillies while the plums are cooking for a sensational Chilli Plum Sauce.*

◆

Originally from tropical America, pawpaw is now grown in most tropical and sub-tropical countries. Pawpaw contains a powerful enzyme which is extracted commercially and used as a meat tenderiser.

Jeannie's Plum Sauce

This is an easy version of the previous sauce: a great hit as a party dip for meatballs.

¼ cup (2 fl oz) chutney (store-bought is fine)
½ cup (4 fl oz) plum jam
1 teaspoon finely chopped (minced) fresh ginger (ginger root)
1 clove garlic, finely chopped (minced)
¼ cup (2 fl oz) malt vinegar

Push the chutney through a sieve, and combine with the other ingredients in a saucepan. Heat gently, stirring frequently. Use immediately or pour into a jar and seal. Serve either hot or cold.

NOTE: *You can also add fresh chopped and seeded chillies for a hot version of this sauce.*

Pressure Cooker (Canner) Plum Chutney

A pressure cooker will speed up the process of making chutney, but some cooking without the lid may still be necessary.

1½ kg (3 lbs) plums, stones (pits) removed and chopped
1 onion, finely chopped (minced)
2 cooking apples, peeled, cored and chopped
½ teaspoon salt
1 teaspoon ground allspice (Jamaican pepper)
3 teaspoons finely chopped (minced) fresh ginger (ginger root)

250 g (½ lb) dates,
stones (pits) removed
1 cup (8 fl oz) malt
vinegar

1 cup (½ lb) sugar

Put all the ingredients into a pressure cooker, cover and pressure cook for 10 minutes. When the pressure reduces, remove the lid. If the chutney is too thin, reduce by cooking uncovered for a few minutes. Spoon into jars and seal.

Makes about 2 kg (4 lb)

Pineapple Chutney

A sweet, spicy chutney that is easy to make using canned pineapple.

1 lemon
2 x 425 g (2 x 1 lb)
cans crushed
pineapple
2 cups (1 lb) brown
sugar
2 cups (16 fl oz) cider
vinegar
2 cups (12 oz)
seedless dark raisins

6 teaspoons finely
chopped (minced)
preserved ginger
1 teaspoon ground
allspice (Jamaican
pepper)
2 cloves
½ teaspoon salt
1 clove garlic, finely
chopped (minced)

Grate the lemon rind and put into a preserving pan. Cut the lemon into thin slices, remove the seeds, then cut the slices into quarters and put into the preserving pan. Add the rest of the ingredients (including the pineapple syrup), bring to the boil, stirring to dissolve the sugar, then simmer for about 30 minutes, stirring frequently, until the mixture is thick. Spoon into jars and seal. Ready to use after a few days.

Makes about 1½ kg (3 lb)

Quince Chutney

2 kg (4 lb) quinces	6 chillies, seeded and
500 g (1 lb) seedless	finely chopped
dark raisins	(minced) (see p. 2)
500 g (1 lb) dates,	500 g (1 lb) brown
stones (pits) removed	sugar
5 cups (40 fl oz)	3 teaspoons mixed
vinegar	mustard (any type)
50 g (2 oz) ground	
ginger	

Cut the quinces into quarters, remove the seeds, and chop finely, but do not peel. Chop the raisins and dates finely. Bring the fruit to the boil in half the vinegar, and simmer until thick. Add the ground ginger and chillies just before removing from the heat and allowing to cool.

In a separate pan, heat the rest of the vinegar with the sugar until it dissolves. Cool, then combine with the quince mixture and stir in the mustard. Do not cook further. Pour into jars and seal. Ready to use in 3 weeks.

Makes about 3 kg (6 lb)

Strawberry Sauce

Sheer bliss with ice-cream or as a filling for tarts.

1 kg (2 lb)	¾ cup (6 fl oz) red
strawberries	wine vinegar
4 cups (2 lb) sugar	

Wash and hull the strawberries. Put the strawberries into a bowl, with the sugar and vinegar, cover and leave for about 6 hours, stirring occasionally. The time is flexible, you can start this sauce in the morning and finish it at night.

Put the strawberries and their juice into a preserving pan and bring to the boil. Boil rapidly for about 15 minutes, stirring occasionally, until it thickens. Leave to cool slightly, about 10 minutes, then pour into jars and seal while still warm.

Makes about 1 kg (2 lb)

Tamarillo (Tree Tomato) Chutney

2 kg (4 lb) tamarillos
(tree tomatoes)
1 red capsicum (bell
or sweet pepper),
seeded and finely
chopped (minced)
500 g (1 lb) frozen
raspberries
1 teaspoon ground
cloves

3 teaspoons salt
3 teaspoons ground
ginger
2 chillies, seeded and
finely chopped
(minced) (see p. 2)
2½ cups (20 fl oz) red
wine vinegar
2 cups (1 lb) sugar

Peel the tamarillos (plunge into boiling water first to make it easy), then chop on a plate to catch the juice. Put into a preserving pan with the capsicum and raspberries, and bring slowly to simmering point. Add the spices and vinegar, and simmer until the mixture starts to reduce, then add the sugar, stirring to dissolve. Continue to cook gently, stirring frequently to prevent sticking, until the mixture thickens. Pour into jars and seal.

Makes about 2½ kg (5 lb)

———— ◆ ————

The tamarillo is native to South America but is widely cultivated elsewhere. It is related to the kiwi fruit and tomato.

Jerusalem Artichoke Relish

Delicious with winter casseroles—should be eaten within a week.

*1½ cups (12 fl oz)
cider vinegar
2 teaspoons salt
½ teaspoon chilli
powder (see p. 2)
1 teaspoon ground
turmeric
½ cup (4 oz) sugar
1 kg (2 lb) Jerusalem
artichokes, peeled
and finely diced*

*2 capsicums (bell or
sweet peppers),
seeded and finely
diced
1 onion, finely
chopped (minced)*

Bring the vinegar to the boil with the salt, chilli powder, turmeric and sugar, and simmer for 5 minutes. Add the vegetables, return to the boil and immediately remove from the heat. Stir to mix well, then spoon into jars. Seal when cool and store in the refrigerator. Ready to eat after 1 day.

Makes about 1½ kg (3 lb)

Carrot Chutney

Delicious on fresh bread with cream cheese.

*1 kg (2 lb) carrots,
washed and scraped
4½ cups (36 fl oz)
malt vinegar
1 cup (8 oz) brown
sugar*

*3 teaspoons finely
chopped (minced) fresh
ginger (ginger root)
1 teaspoon ground
allspice (Jamaican
pepper)*

Grate the carrots and put into a preserving pan with the other ingredients. Bring to the boil and simmer for 20-30 minutes until the mixture is thick and all the liquid has evaporated. Pour into jars and seal.

Makes about 1 kg (2 lb)

Capsicum (Bell or Sweet Pepper) Chutney

250 g (8 oz) onions
¼ cup (2 fl oz) olive oil
2 red capsicums (bell or sweet peppers), seeded
500 g (1 lb) tomatoes, peeled and chopped
2 cloves garlic, finely chopped (minced)
½ teaspoon salt
1 teaspoon grated fresh ginger (ginger root)
1 cup (8 oz) sugar
½ cup (4 fl oz) red wine vinegar

Finely chop (mince) the onions and saute in the olive oil, in a preserving pan, until soft. Dice the capsicums and add to the onion. After 5 minutes, add the tomatoes, garlic, salt and ginger, stir, and after another 10 minutes add the sugar and vinegar. Stir well. Cover and cook on very low heat for about 1 hour. Keeps for about 3 weeks in the fridge. Serve at room temperature.

Makes about 1 kg (2 lb)

Celery Relish

Sweet and crunchy with bread and cheese.

1 head of celery	*1 teaspoon salt*
3 tomatoes, peeled	*½ teaspoon mustard*
and chopped	*powder*
1 capsicum (bell or	*1 teaspoon dried*
sweet pepper), seeded	*celery seeds*
and diced	*1 cup (8 fl oz) cider*
¼ cup (2 oz) sugar	*vinegar*

Wash and string the celery, then chop finely. Put into a preserving pan with the other ingredients. Bring to the boil, then simmer for 1 hour, stirring occasionally, until thick. Spoon into jars and seal.

Makes about 1 kg (2 lb)

Choko (Chayote, Christophene) Chutney

2 kg (4 lb) chokos	*500 g (1 lb) onions,*
(chayotes,	*finely chopped*
christophenes)	*(minced)*
¼ cup (2 oz) salt	*1 cup (8 fl oz) water*
2.5 cm (1 inch) piece	*1½ cups (8 oz)*
fresh ginger	*sultanas (golden*
(ginger root)	*raisins)*
3 teaspoons crushed	*2 cups (1 lb) sugar*
dry chillies (see p. 2)	*7 cups (56 fl oz) malt*
3 teaspoons	*vinegar*
peppercorns	
700 g (1½ lb) green	
apples, peeled, cored	
and diced	

Peel the chokos under running water (juices can affect the skin) and dice. Layer the chokos in a bowl, sprinkling each layer with salt. Cover with a clean tea towel and set aside overnight. Drain. Rinse in cold water and drain again.

Tie the spices in a muslin (cheesecloth) bag and put into a cooking pan with the choko, apples, onions and water. Heat gently, then simmer until the vegetables are tender. Add the sultanas, sugar and vinegar. Bring to the boil, stirring constantly. Cook until thickened. Remove the bag of spices. Pour into jars and seal.

Makes about 3 kg (6 lb)

Corn Relish

4½ cups (36 fl oz) cider vinegar
1 cup (8 oz) sugar
1 teaspoon salt
1 teaspoon ground cinnamon
6 teaspoons mustard powder
500 g (1 lb) white cabbage, finely chopped (shredded)

2 onions, finely chopped (minced)
3 capsicums (bell or sweet) peppers, seeded and finely chopped (shredded)
1 kg (2 lb) corn kernels, fresh, tinned or frozen

Put the vinegar, sugar and spices into a preserving pan and bring to the boil. Add all the other ingredients, return to the boil and simmer for about 1 hour, stirring frequently, until the mixture is thick. Pour into jars and seal.

Makes about 2 kg (4 lb)

Hot Chilli Sauce

A little goes a long way. Handle the chillies with care—wear rubber gloves and seed them outdoors, or do it under running water.

225 g (½ lb) fresh
  chillies, seeded
  (see p. 2)
1 medium onion,
  chopped
2 cloves garlic
4-5 tablespoons
  grated green
  pawpaw (papaya)

1 teaspoon salt
2 teaspoons sugar
½ cup (4 fl oz) malt
  vinegar

Put all ingredients into a food processor and puree. Pour the puree into a saucepan, bring to the boil and simmer for a few minutes. Pour into jars and seal.

Makes about 375 g (12 oz)

Eggplant (Aubergine) and Chilli Pepper Relish

¼ cup (2 fl oz)
  vegetable oil
2 teaspoons black
  mustard seeds
4 medium-sized
  eggplants
  (aubergines), sliced
1 stalk lemon grass
10 fresh chillies (see
  p. 2)
2 teaspoons Chinese
  five-spice powder

4 cloves garlic, finely
  chopped (minced)
2 teaspoons finely
  chopped (minced)
  fresh ginger
  (ginger root)
2 teaspoons salt
2 cups (16 fl oz) malt
  vinegar

Heat the oil and fry the mustard seeds until they start to pop, then add the eggplant slices, lemon grass, whole chillies, Chinese five-spice powder, garlic and ginger, and fry gently in oil until cooked, but not browned. Stir in the salt and vinegar, bring to the boil, then remove from the heat. Pack into jars and seal when cold.

Makes about 1 kg (2 lb)

Fresh Herb Sauce

A blend of fresh herbs that enhances the flavour of fish or more delicately flavoured meat such as veal—try it with char-grilled veal cutlets (chops) or barbecued chicken breasts.

1 large bunch of mixed herbs (about 2 cups of leaves)— whatever you have growing in the garden, but parsley is a good start
2 cloves garlic
3 teaspoons drained capers

3 teaspoons Dijon mustard
3 teaspoons lemon juice (or wine vinegar)
1 cup (8 fl oz) olive oil
Salt and freshly ground black pepper

Remove coarse stems from the herbs, then process in a food processor with the garlic, capers, mustard and lemon juice. Gradually add the olive oil until the mixture is thick and smooth. Season with salt and pepper. Keep in the fridge, but serve at room temperature.

Makes about 500 g (1 lb)

———— ◆ ————

The eggplant was originally egg-like both in shape and colour (hence the English name).

Pesto Sauce

This famous sauce, which originated in Genoa, is traditionally served with pasta and gnocchi (stir room-temperature pesto through hot pasta or gnocchi—do not heat further) but it can also be used in a lot of other ways. Try it in soup, on jacket-baked potatoes, as a dip for cherry tomatoes or lamb kebabs (shish kabobs), or mixed with dried tomatoes and cheese as a filling for savoury tarts.

100 g (4 oz) fresh basil leaves
3 cloves garlic, peeled
50 g (2 oz) pine nuts or walnuts

50 g (2 oz) freshly grated Parmesan
1 cup (8 fl oz) olive oil
Freshly ground black pepper

Process the basil, garlic, pine nuts or walnuts, and Parmesan in a food processor. Slowly add the oil until the sauce is thick and smooth. Season with black pepper. Scrape into a jar and keep in the fridge—also freezes.

Makes about 500 g (1 lb)

Sherry Peppers Sauce

In the Caribbean you can buy this sauce already bottled—but it's easy to make your own. Use it to spark up anything from scrambled eggs to seafood chowder.

10 chillies (you can
use more or less as
you please, but it
should be very
hot—see p. 2)

2 cups (16 fl oz) dry
sherry

Put the chillies into a jar or bottle and add the sherry. Seal. Leave for 2 weeks. If you wish, you can strain off the chillies before using the sauce.

Makes about 2 cups (16 fl oz)

Pumpkin (Winter Squash) Chutney

1 kg (2 lb) cubes of
pumpkin (winter
squash), roughly
chopped
4 tomatoes, skinned
and chopped
225 g (8 oz) onions,
chopped
¼ cup (2 oz) sultanas
(golden raisins)
½ kg (1 lb) soft dark
brown sugar

2 teaspoons salt
2 teaspoons finely
chopped (minced)
fresh ginger
(ginger root)
1 teaspoon black
pepper
2 teaspoons nutmeg
2 cloves garlic,
chopped
2 cups (16 fl oz)
vinegar

Put all the ingredients into a preserving pan, bring slowly to the boil and simmer for about 1 hour. As the chutney thickens, stir constantly to prevent sticking to the bottom. Pour into jars, cover and seal.

Makes about 1½ kg (3 lb)

Chow-chow

1 cup (6 oz) red
    kidney beans, soaked
    overnight in water
    and drained
2 capsicums (bell or
    sweet peppers),
    seeded and sliced
½ cauliflower
    separated into florets
225 g (8 oz) French
    beans (green bean,
    haricot vert),
    trimmed and sliced

100 g (4 oz) frozen or
    tinned corn kernels
2 cups (16 fl oz)
    vinegar
½ cup (4 oz) soft
    brown sugar
6 teaspoons mustard
    powder
1 teaspoon curry
    powder (see p. 2)

Cook the vegetables separately in boiling, salted water until they are just tender, and drain. Combine the vinegar, sugar, mustard and curry powder in a preserving pan, bring to the boil, stirring to dissolve the sugar. Add the vegetables and simmer for a few minutes. Spoon into jars and seal.

Makes about 1½ kg (3 lb)

Green Tomato Chutney

2 kg (4 lb) green
    tomatoes, chopped
2 onions, finely
    chopped (minced)
1 apple, peeled,
    cored and chopped
2 fresh chillies,
    seeded and chopped
    (see p. 2)
1 teaspoon cayenne
    pepper

1 teaspoon salt
1 cup treacle
    (molasses)
½ cup (4 oz) soft,
    brown sugar
1 cup (8 fl oz) malt
    vinegar
3 teaspoons finely
    chopped (minced)
    fresh ginger
    (ginger root)

½ teaspoon ground
cloves

1 teaspoon ground
cinnamon

Combine all ingredients in a preserving pan, bring slowly to the boil and simmer, stirring occasionally, until thick (about 2 hours). Pour into jars and seal.

Makes about 2 kg (4 lb)

Rachael's Hot Tomato Chutney

3 oranges
2 kg (4 lb) ripe
  tomatoes
2½ cups (20 fl oz)
  malt vinegar
1 kg (2 lb) sugar
Juice of 4 limes or
  lemons
500 g (1 lb) sultanas
  (golden raisins)
100 g (4 oz) finely
  chopped (minced)
  fresh ginger
  (ginger root)

100 g (4 oz) finely
  chopped (minced)
  garlic
25 g (1 oz) chilli
  powder (see p. 2)
6 teaspoons salt
1 cinnamon stick
6 cloves

Finely peel the orange rind, then cut it into thin strips. Chop the tomatoes and cook in a preserving pan until soft. Sieve with a little of the vinegar to remove the seeds and skin. Put the tomato pulp back into the pan with the sugar and the lime or lemon juice. Cook until the mixture thickens, then add the sultanas, ginger, garlic, chilli powder, salt and remaining vinegar. Cook slowly, stirring thoroughly, until the mixture starts to thicken, then add the cinnamon and cloves. Keep stirring until the mixture is thick. Add the orange peel just before removing from the stove. Pour into jars and seal.

Makes about 2½ kg (5 lb)

Tomato Chutney

1½ kg (3 lb) tomatoes
500 g (1 lb) dates,
  stones (pits)
  removed, chopped
1 teaspoon chilli
  powder (see p. 2)
3 cloves garlic,
  chopped

3 teaspoons finely
  chopped (minced)
  fresh ginger
  (ginger root)
1 teaspoon salt
¾ cup (6 oz) brown sugar
4 cups (32 fl oz) malt
  vinegar

Plunge the tomatoes into boiling water, remove the skins, and chop. Put into a preserving pan with the other ingredients, and bring to the boil. Simmer on low heat, stirring occasionally, until thickened, about two hours. Pour into jars and seal.

Makes about 1½ kg (3 lb)

Peg Bowden's Tomato Sauce

5 kg (10 lb) tomatoes,
  roughly chopped
1 kg (2 lb) apples,
  cored and chopped
1 kg (2 lb) onions,
  chopped
100 g (4 oz) salt
16 cloves garlic,
  finely chopped
  (minced)
5 cups (40 fl oz)
  vinegar

3 teaspoons cloves
3 teaspoons allspice
  berries (Jamaican
  peppers)
3 teaspoons ground
  ginger
3 teaspoons cayenne
  pepper
4 cups (2 lb) sugar

Put all the ingredients, except the sugar, into a preserving pan, bring to the boil and simmer until thick. Sieve, then return to the pan with the sugar, bring to the boil and simmer for 1 hour, stirring regularly to prevent sticking. Pour into bottles and seal.

Makes about 6 kg (12 lb)

Tomato Salsa

This is a useful basic sauce to have in the fridge.

1 kg (2 lb) tomatoes	*2 cloves garlic, finely*
¼ cup (2 fl oz) olive	*chopped (minced)*
oil	*Salt and black*
1 teaspoon sugar	*pepper*

Plunge the tomatoes into boiling water, remove the skins, seed and chop finely. Put into a preserving pan and cook over low heat, stirring occasionally, until the mixture starts to thicken. Stir in the other ingredients. Cook, stirring occasionally, for 10 minutes. Will keep in the fridge for 3 weeks.

Makes about 1 kg (2 lb)

Green Tomato Relish

1½ kg (3 lb) green tomatoes, sliced	2½ cups (20 fl oz) malt vinegar
500 g (1 lb) vegetable marrow (summer squash), peeled and diced	1 teaspoon mustard powder
¼ cup (2 oz) salt	1 teaspoon ground allspice (Jamaican pepper)
1 capsicum (bell or sweet pepper)	½ teaspoon curry powder
4 cloves garlic, crushed	½ teaspoon caraway seeds

Layer the tomatoes and marrow in a bowl, sprinkling each layer with salt. Cover the bowl with a clean tea towel and set aside overnight.

Next day, drain the tomatoes and marrow and put into a pan. Wash the capsicum, remove the seeds, dice finely, and add to the pan with the garlic. Mix the vinegar with the spices, then add this mixture to the pan. Bring slowly to the boil then simmer, uncovered, stirring occasionally, until the vegetables are tender and the liquid reduced and thickening. This will take about 1 hour. Pour into jars and seal. Best after 3 months.

Makes about 2 kg (4 lb)

———— ◆ ————

Turnips come in a variety of shapes and sizes and the skins are generally yellow-orange, white, green or tinged with purple.

Chilli Tomato Sauce

2 kg (4 lb) tomatoes	2 cups (17 fl oz) malt
2 large onions, finely	vinegar
chopped (minced)	3 teaspoons finely
½ cup (4 oz) sugar	chopped (minced),
3 teaspoons salt	seeded chillies (see p. 2)

Plunge the tomatoes into boiling water, then remove the skins and chop finely. Combine with all the other ingredients in a preserving pan and bring to the boil. Simmer, stirring occasionally, until the mixture thickens. Pour into jars and seal.

Makes about 2 kg (4 lb)

Turnip Chutney

Excellent with roast duck.

1 kg (2 lb) turnips,	2 cups (16 fl oz) cider
peeled and roughly	vinegar
chopped	100 g (4 oz) seedless
½ kg (1 lb) apples,	dark raisins
peeled, cored and	1 cup (8 oz) sugar
diced	1 teaspoon ground
½ kg (1 lb) onions,	black pepper
finely chopped	1 teaspoon salt
(minced)	¼ cup (2 fl oz)
1 teaspoon curry	Golden Syrup (light
powder (see p. 2)	treacle, corn syrup)

Cook the turnips in boiling salted water for 20 minutes or until tender. Drain and mash. Put all the ingredients, except the Golden Syrup, into a preserving pan and bring slowly to the boil, stirring until the sugar has dissolved. Add the Golden Syrup and stir. Simmer gently, stirring frequently, until the chutney thickens—about 1 hour. Pour into jars and seal.

Makes about 2 kg (4 lb)

INSTANT CHUTNEYS

Throughout Asia chutneys are often made on the spur of the moment to accompany a meal.

Instant Apple Chutney

Delicious with char-grilled duck or pork as well as curries.

*4 Granny Smith
(large, green) apples,
peeled and grated
(shredded)
3 teaspoons salt
½ cup grated
(shredded) fresh
coconut
(desiccated (flaked)
can be used if
necessary)*

*1 small onion, finely
chopped (minced)
45 ml (1½ fl oz)
lemon juice*

Sprinkle the grated apple with the salt, leave for 10 minutes and drain. Combine with the remaining ingredients. Store in the refrigerator.

Makes about 500 g (1 lb)

Coconut Chutney

A traditional accompaniment to Indian food, but very adaptable. Try it with vegetable fritters, savoury meatballs, deep-fried seafood . . .

*1 lemon
2 chillies, seeded
(see p. 2)
¼ cup (2 oz) chopped,
fresh coriander leaves
1 small red (Italian)
onion, roughly
chopped*

*1 teaspoon salt
2 teaspoons ground
cumin
1 teaspoon black
mustard seeds
½ cup (4 oz)
desiccated (flaked)
coconut*

Remove the peel and pith from the lemon, cut into pieces and remove the seeds. Put into a food processor with the other ingredients, except the coconut, and blend to a puree. Add the coconut gradually, scraping down the sides of the processor and adding a little water if necessary. Scrape into a bowl and store in the fridge—best served the same day.

Makes about 250 g (8 oz)

Fresh Coconut Chutney

When fresh coconuts are available at the market this is one of the interesting ways you can use them. It's wonderful with barbecued chicken, especially if the chicken has been marinated in Asian spices.

1 cup (8 oz) freshly grated (shredded) coconut
45 ml (1½ fl oz) milk from the coconut
4 green chillies, seeded and finely chopped (minced) (see p. 2)
3-4 tablespoons finely chopped (minced) fresh mint
3-4 tablespoons finely chopped (minced) fresh coriander
45 ml (1½ fl oz) fresh lime juice
30 ml (1 fl oz) vegetable oil

Process all ingredients in a blender or food processor. Store in the refrigerator.

Makes about 375 g (12 oz)

——— ◆ ———

The fruit of the coconut palm requires a full year to ripen. Marco Polo was one of the first Europeans to describe coconuts.

Instant Apricot Chutney

Incredibly easy to make—good with pan-fried fish.

225 g (8 oz) apricot
    jam
1 onion, finely
    chopped (minced)
1 capsicum (bell or
    sweet pepper), seeded
    and finely chopped
    (minced)

¼ cup (2 fl oz) white
    wine vinegar
1 teaspoon ground
    allspice (Jamaican
    pepper)
1 teaspoon ground
    ginger
½ teaspoon salt

Mix all ingredients together and spoon into a jar. Store in the refrigerator and use within a week.

Makes about 500 g (1 lb)

Cucumber and Mint Chutney

Good packed into pita pockets with spicy meatballs or chicken kebabs (shish kabobs).

1 cucumber, peeled,
    seeded and finely
    chopped (minced)
2 tablespoons finely
    chopped (minced)
    fresh mint

1 teaspoon ground
    cumin
½ cup (4 oz) yoghurt
    (yogurt)

Combine all the ingredients—a little lemon juice can be added if desired. Store in the refrigerator, but serve at room temperature. Should be used the day it's made.

Makes about 250 g (8 oz)

Coriander Chutney

You can adapt this recipe to make a very good mint chutney, by substituting mint for coriander.

*1 bunch coriander—
  enough to fill about
  1 cup firmly packed
  with leaves
1 onion, finely
  chopped (minced)
1 green chilli, seeded
  (see p. 2)
1 teaspoon finely
  chopped (minced)
  fresh ginger
  (ginger root)*

*3 teaspoons
  desiccated (flaked)
  coconut
1 teaspoon salt
1 teaspoon sugar
45 ml (1½ fl oz) malt
  vinegar*

Put all the ingredients, except the vinegar, into a blender or food processor and puree. Add the vinegar gradually, until well blended. Scrape into a jar and store in the refrigerator.

Makes about 250 g (8 oz)

Fresh Mango Chutney

This uncooked chutney is best made close to serving time—perfect with cold seafood.

2 mangoes
2 chillies, seeded and
*   finely chopped*
*   (minced) (see p. 2)*
2 teaspoons finely
*   chopped (minced)*
*   fresh ginger*
*   (ginger root)*

1 small onion, finely
*   chopped (minced)*
3 teaspoons white
*   wine vinegar*
1 teaspoon sugar
½ teaspoon salt
3 teaspoons mint,
*   finely chopped*

Peel the mangoes, remove the stones (pits) and slice. Put into a bowl and mash with a fork, then mix in the other ingredients. If making ahead, keep in the refrigerator.

Makes about 500 g (1 lb)

Peanut Chutney

Another instant chutney to serve with Asian food or as a dip.

1 bunch coriander—
*   enough to fill about*
*   1 cup firmly packed*
*   with leaves*
1 cup salted peanuts
2 green chillies,
*   seeded (see p. 2)*

2½ cm (1 inch) piece
*   fresh ginger*
*   (ginger root),*
*   roughly chopped*
1 teaspoon sugar
Yoghurt (yogurt)—
*   about ½ cup (4 oz)*

Process all ingredients, except the yoghurt, in a blender or food processor, then gradually add enough yoghurt to make a moist paste. Store in refrigerator—use within 3 days.

Makes about 500 g (1 lb)

Walnut Chutney

100 g (4 oz) walnuts,   1 teaspoon salt
   shelled   ¹/₃ cup (2½ oz) yoghurt
2 chillies, seeded   (yogurt)
   (see p. 2)

Process the walnuts, chillies and salt in blender or food processor and gradually add the yoghurt to make a paste—use more yoghurt if necessary. Store in the refrigerator—use within 3 days.

Makes about 250 g (8 oz)

$\mathscr{I}$NDEX